The Paradox of Success:

Why Success Sucks, and 15 Other Curiosities of Confidence, Happiness, and Healing

Tamsen E. Taylor, Ph.D.
Tamsen Connects

For Tommy - and everyone else who knows we are all connected.

Release date: June 25, 2022

Find additional resources related to the book at
https://tamsenconnects.com/paradox

Tamsen Connects
Guelph, Ontario, Canada
https://www.tamsenconnects.com

Catalogue data available from Library and Archives Canada

ISBN 978-1-9991748-0-4 (Paperback)

ISBN 978-1-9991748-1-1 (EPUB)

Contents

The Problem

The trouble with the rat race is that even if you win, you're still a rat.

- Lily Tomlin

Have you ever felt like you won the rat race - but somehow you still lost?

You feel you still ARE lost?

If you've checked off all the boxes of the "rat race" - you've gotten the respected education, the fab career, the spouse everyone envies, the dream house, the super adorable 2.5 kids, the mischievous yet mostly obedient dog - yet you still feel a pit in your stomach and a deep dissatisfaction - this book was written for you.

Of course - you SHOULDN'T feel miserable, right?! You can't think of a single person who has it better.

No one has it Better... Except...

You think of that wild and crazy friend of yours, who after you finished school together, she dropped a high powered legal career to take off and weave ponchos in a yurt somewhere. She has almost no money, almost no stuff, she's single (er - on and off), and along the way she somehow "forgot" to have kids - but last you heard from her, she seemed... Happy. Giddy, even.

Shouldn't YOU be the one who can't stop chuckling because of how amazing YOUR life is? Somehow, you're successful - but your success SUCKS. You're confused about why. After all, you did everything RIGHT. You love your kids. You love your partner. You love your career - mostly. And you're freaking fantastic at it. Due for a promotion any day!

The fact that the biggest stress in your life right now is that little Robin hates math and you worry she might not get into your alma mater doesn't really quite seem like enough to explain why you feel so...Helpless. Hopeless.

Trapped.

You're Successful - but You're not Feeling it

You feel more than a little angry - dammit! - because you've done all the right things, you've paid your dues. You've not only towed the line, you've excelled! Sometimes you're angry at the world - because it's not FAIR that you've done what you've been told would make you happy and feel miserable. And sometimes

- especially at 3am - you're angry at YOURSELF. Because what's WRONG with you anyway!?!?!

So, you're lucky, you're privileged, your ducks are in a row - And sometimes you're miserable, and you don't feel like you have the right to be. Here's something to consider: Doing what's expected, what you're told - is often the safer and easier option. It's predictable. It gets you acceptance. And you don't have to go through the discomfort and work of figuring stuff out for yourself.

But focusing on meeting other people's expectations is likely what's gotten you where you are. "Successful" - and miserable.

If You Feel Successful - and Miserable - You're not Alone

Many women when they find themselves here feel shame. They feel like everyone else is happy and has things figured out, and they're somehow broken.

I've interviewed many people for my Momtellectual podcast, and most of them have gone through a "crucible moment" - a time of stress and change, when they realized they had the power to - and WANTED to - change their life and have a different future than they had planned. They wanted a life different than the life they had been told would make them successful and happy.

Like Caryn Gillen (Choosing Your Story, Momtellectual Episode 134 - find it at tamsen.ca/momtellectual 134), who pursued an education to qualify as a psychotherapist because it was more in line with what she was told about "success" than being a life coach - who then had the insight to realize that a life coach was what she really WANTED to be, where her interests and talents lay. And she was brave enough to make the change.

It's important to know we're not alone in struggling to feel successful, even when we "have it all". Here are some other stories:

Like me, Dona Bumgarner wanted to be a mom for a long time, and also found "mom life" to not be at all what she expected. She committed herself to being a stay-at-home mom and learned how to cook, get stains out of the laundry, and taught her daughter baby sign language. Though she was convinced she "should" be happy, instead she felt suffocated by her life. Her plans were derailed when she was diagnosed with an aggressive form of breast cancer, forcing her to put the brakes on and make serious changes. She's now built a life she loves, and she's a life coach helping other moms make important changes so they can find joy in their lives, preferably before something like a major health scare! (Find what You Need, Momtellectual episode 137 - find it at tamsen.ca/momtellectual137).

Shawna Percy had a career, was married to a man she loved very much, and was the mom of a wonderful almost two-year-old daughter - but behind the scenes she was struggling with her own mental health issues when her husband died by suicide. As she puts it - "Not everything happens for a reason - but everything can be redeemed." She redeemed the loss of her husband by dedicating herself to preventing suicide. Shawna is now a Certified Suicide Intervention Trainer, and runs mental health and suicide prevention workshops through her organization Life Voice. (Suicide Intervention, Momtellectual episode 67 - find it at tamsen.ca/momtellectual67).

Janette Hargreaves redefined successful parenting for herself, and broke her yelling habit. She used her own experience to shift her career and is now a parenting coach supporting other parents who want to choose a different version of parenting for themselves and their children (Breaking the Cycle, Momtellectual Episode 130 - find it at tamsen.ca/momtellectual130).

The main point is this - for you to truly FEEL successful, YOU need to define what success is to YOU. Make it personal. Like your friend in her yurt did.

If you're ready to make that change, read on.

Loving the ideal more than the reality is the cause of all the misery the human species creates for itself.

- Dean Koontz

It's Time for a Change

> Not everything that is faced can be changed, but nothing can be changed until it is faced.
>
> - Lucille Ball

Are you struggling?

Do you hesitate to take even a moment to examine your life, because it's scary - you get that feeling - is THIS all there is? THIS is supposed to be success?

Instead of poking at that pain like a tongue worrying at a throbbing tooth, let's move on to how to make changes so you can FEEL successful.

This book is a distillation of the advice and wisdom I've come across through research, in interviews with truly successful women, and from my own experience living a "successful" but dissatisfying life and coming through the other side.

And here's the thing... You need to figure out what success means to YOU.

Define Success for Yourself

A big chunk of finding the right answers is asking useful questions.

Instead of thinking of this as a book that "has all the answers" - I'm inviting you on a journey that will help you find your own answers. Realize that taking the time and doing your best to ANSWER the questions that are asked here is an important part of the work.

And as you read this book and answer the questions I ask in it, please also practice self-compassion and treat yourself with kindness.

Self-compassion is important enough there's a whole chapter on it (Curiosity #2 - The Paradox of Self-Compassion) - but for now, realize that it might take time and work to find clear answers, and that those answers are very likely to change over time and with other changes in your life. Do your best to be ok with that.

In this book you'll find important pieces of information you're probably missing, as well as questions that invite you to personalize these ideas and help you to put these ideas into practice in your life.

Questioning What You've Been Told Gets Uncomfortable

Yes, some of the questions you ask yourself might feel uncomfortable. It might take awhile to come up with an answer that feels helpful - and it may be challenging to face some things.

But you know what? It can also be FUN!

You may be on this journey because you are struggling and really need a change. You may be here because you believe (like me) that personal growth can be interesting and a lifelong adventure. Either way, there can be some hard parts, but working on our emotional health should also feel GOOD sometimes, right!?!?! So, let's dive in and question one strategy that a lot of us have used to feel better that often backfires, so we can pave the way for more useful strategies.

Have you ever tried to dismiss your feelings, and talk yourself out of feeling bad?

Don't Dismiss Your Feelings

We can feel pain and feel privileged at the same time. Conflicting emotions like pain and privilege can lead us to feeling like we don't "deserve" to need help, to talk to people about our painful feelings - or to even feel bad at all.

Here's something to think about:

> Truth Bomb: There are no Pain Olympics. **Everyone experiences pain, and no one's pain is more "worthy".**

Would it change how you deal with your pain - and other people's - if you realize that it's not helpful to treat pain like a competitive sport? Are you in the habit of telling yourself you shouldn't feel miserable, angry, or afraid, because other people have it worse? How many times have you had someone try to help you by saying "At least...." Did that really feel supportive? We'll talk a lot about how to give and receive healthy emotional support in Curiosity #8 - The Paradox of Support, but for now, let's consider the role of comparison in logic versus emotion.

We're Taught to Value Logic Over Emotion

Logically, comparisons are possible. When we use our "logical brain" - it can make a lot of sense to compare. Many of our words are all about comparison - is it bigger than a bread box? Larger, smaller, taller, shorter, all of those words are meaningless unless we know what is being compared.

Emotions give us a totally different kind of information. Emotions are a viscerally felt part of our experience - and it's impossible to know if we feel the same as anyone else. No one deserves to have painful feelings more than anyone else, no matter what our logic might say.

Instead of trying to compete in the Pain Olympics, let's try agreeing that emotional pain sucks. It's painful! Emotional pain is also useful, and it is intended to give you some information that could save your life. Many of the topics in this book involve discussing the benefits of being more aware of and connected to our emotions, and how to balance that without feeling like we're being swallowed whole by pain. One of the beginning steps to connecting with our feelings is that we need to respect our feelings, whatever we feel.

We'll deal with emotional health and how to increase your sense of well-being in a lot more detail in the Happiness chapter (Curiosity #3 - The Happiness Myth) but for now, focus on the fact that you deserve to have your feelings, whatever they are. I encourage you to bring your complete self on the journey to feeling successful, including all of your feelings.

How this Book is Organized:

This book is divided into several sections.

In section 1 we'll question "success" - we'll talk about what success is, what it isn't, and why it sometimes sucks to be successful.

In the next three sections, I'll challenge you to think about what success means to you personally in several different areas of your life: your relationship with yourself (section 2, Creating Self-Worth), your relationships with other people (section 3, Creating Healthy Relationships), and your connection to purpose and meaning (section 4, Creating Meaning).

Once you figure some of that stuff out, in section 5 we'll pull it all together and you can start redefining success - not only into something that will genuinely FEEL successful to you - but something that you will be able to feel every day, not work toward sometime in the distant future.

So let's look at the Paradox of Success - why success sometimes sucks, and what to do about it.

But first, welcome to the questions you'll find at the end of every chapter. The "Five Growing Questions" are questions that can help you learn more about yourself so you can gather the information you need to create your personal definition of success. If you want to get the most out of this book, take some time to put your answers to these questions into words, whether written or spoken. You'll find that putting your thoughts into words will help you get clarity and gain understanding.

Once you have finished answering the growing questions, take some time to consider what you have learned from this chapter, and answer the summary question. Decide what you would like to bring from this chapter into your personal definition of success. Don't worry about choosing something "right", huge, or magically profound. Focus on choosing something that you might find helpful on your success journey. Also don't worry about how exactly you'll include it, we'll be figuring that out later.

To help you keep your answers together and organized, I've put together the questions as a separate journal. You can find out how to download that journal for free at http://tamsen.ca/paradoxjournalfree. If you already journal, then you know that journalling about these questions could be really powerful. And if you don't already have a journalling practice, I recommend trying it out. If you'd like help getting started, you can find my

Journalling Jumpstart program here - http://tamsen.ca/journallingjumpstart.

Five Growing Questions about Comparison:

1. How do you use comparisons to deal with emotional discomfort? What words do you use?

2. Do you believe that it's possible to be in pain and grateful at the same time? Why or why not?

3. Describe a time you had feelings that surprised you. What did you expect to feel? What did you feel instead? What does that comparison (real vs. expected feelings) bring up for you?

4. If you tell someone about a problem you're having, and they say "Well, at least....", what feelings does that bring up for you?

5. Spend some time asking yourself about whether you respect both the information you get from logic/thinking and the information you get from your emotions. How do these sources of information compare?

Change Summary Question:

What was one thing you learned in this chapter about making a change that you want to include in your personal definition of success? Write or dictate a note for yourself, or put it in the appropriate section of the journal provided (find out how to download the journal for free at http://tamsen.ca/paradoxjournalfree).

> Always remember that you are absolutely unique. Just like everyone else.
>
> - Margaret Mead

Section: Questioning "Success"

Reconsider your definitions. We are prone to judge success by the index of our salaries or the size of our automobiles rather than by the quality of our service and relationship to mankind.

- Dr. Martin Luther King, Jr.

Before we jump into making our success personal and redefining it, it's useful to look at how we got into this mess in the first place. In this section, we'll talk about why success became a paradox for so many of us. Take some time to answer these orienting questions to see where you're at right now, and to get your goals clear enough that you can write them down.

Success Orienting Questions:

1. Definition question: What does "success" mean to you right now?

2. Self-assessment question: What is your current level of success?

3. Goal question: What is the main thing you want to change about your level of success?

4. Achievement question: How will you know you've achieved your success goal?

> For many men, the acquisition of wealth does not end their troubles, it only changes them.
>
> - Seneca

The Paradox of Success

I think everybody should get rich and famous and do everything they ever dreamed of so that they can see that it's not the answer.

- Jim Carrey

I was finally going to be happy!

I have always wanted to have children. After 3 years of fertility treatments and 3 miscarriages, I was finally expecting a baby boy, and far enough along in my pregnancy that my doctor said losing him was unlikely. I had what I had worked so hard for.

Success! I could be happy now.

But wait - the doctors said that my baby dying was unlikely, but I couldn't stop being afraid. And then I had a huge bleeding episode just when I was supposed to be "safe" from my son dying. I guess I was just going to be terrified for now, but I could be happy once my son was born, and here, safe and healthy. I'm waiting a bit longer to be happy. But it's coming!

Yay, he's here! He's born, and alive, and nothing seems to be horribly wrong. I'm even recovering ok.

Success! I could be happy now.

Successful and Miserable

But wait - I'm exhausted. Breastfeeding mostly sucks, if you can excuse the pun. I feel trapped, since my son wants to be nursing 23 hours out of every 24, and I found it too awkward to try to nurse while moving around.

I'm also still terrified - babies don't just die during pregnancy, there's also SIDS. There are horror shows that play in my mind, like me falling as I'm walking with him, and squashing him to death. Like us getting into an accident when we're in the car, and my son dying. Like my son getting some incurable illness, suffering horribly, and dying. On and on.

But I achieved my goal! I'm successful! I have that thing that was supposed to make me happy. The only thing that was holding me back from being happy was not having a child, and now I have my son, and...

And I was still miserable.

I thought all those people who said new moms don't have time to shower were exaggerating. Nope. I thought that there might be something approaching normal sleep. I didn't realize that "sleep when the baby sleeps" meant for 10 minutes at a time. Never mind that my son wouldn't sleep unless he was being held, and I was too petrified to co-sleep with him. I thought it was also an exaggeration that most conversations would revolve around poop. Various bodily fluids were the main topic of conversation for quite a long time.

I thought that I would never feel lonely. After all, I had my baby with me All. The. Time. Yet I can't remember a time I felt lonelier and more isolated.

I thought I was ready for this - and I didn't expect how sometimes the seemingly small things could make me feel like a really, really, horrible mother. You know, like not being happy and grateful every second.

> That's the paradox of success - we're taught acquiring and achieving certain things will make us feel successful and happy, but **getting what we've been taught we should want often results in us feeling LESS happy and successful.**

But...I ASKED for this!

Problem was, all that stuff that came with having a newborn was NORMAL. All the stuff that I wanted to complain about? I ASKED for this. This is supposed to be natural - what could be more natural than being a mom?

I was feeling absolutely incompetent in the role I wanted to be the most successful in. So, then I wasn't only miserable, I was self- judgy, telling myself that I'm wrong for feeling how I feel. And also? I was SUPER confused. I did everything that I was supposed to do to be happy, and it didn't work. What the heck am I supposed to do now?

I felt broken. And stupid. And very alone.

Why does Success SUCK?

When we finally get what we want, the things that are supposed to make us happy, we find we still have ALL our feelings - including the painful ones. Many of us find getting the thing we thought we wanted isn't the experience we expected or hoped for - and now we're not only still not happy, we're left adrift not knowing what to do next.

As is true of my story about having my son, there is often also shame with being successful but not happy. We feel the need to hide, like no one would understand. We did this to ourselves, after all. And since the thing we achieved is something that we said would make us happy, that society in general and our friends and family also expected to make us happy, we don't know where to go for support to deal with healing our painful feelings.

We won the rat race, but we're not happy being rats. What next?

It helps to understand why "success" can suck - and to realize you're not alone in experiencing these things. Here are five possibilities that came up for me in my own journey and in my conversations with other women who have gone through this.

See if any of these reasons why success can leave you feeling unsuccessful hit home for you.

#1 - Any Change is a Loss of the Familiar

I think that it's important for us to recognize that even "good" changes - the changes that happen when you're successful, when you get what you thought you wanted - are still experiences that involve LOSS.

Loss of the familiar is still loss.

Losses naturally can bring forward all sorts of feelings, even contradictory or unexpected ones. Change means things are unpredictable, you don't quite know what to expect anymore. And because many people are afraid when things are unfamiliar, change often brings fear along for the ride.

It might help if those feelings of loss and fear weren't totally unexpected.

Often, like with many people experiencing new parenthood, even if it's something that they really wanted, it's still HARD. Acknowledging that it's a huge change, and that there might be some painful feelings as well as joyful ones can help people who are suffering feel safe to express what they're feeling. Feeling pain doesn't mean that you don't also feel joy and gratitude.

#2 - Success can Bring Unexpected Consequences.

Say you got that promotion you were angling for.

Congratulations! Success!

But now your work relationships are awkward because your best work friend also wanted the promotion and now they're angry and badmouthing you. Your partner is disappointed and critical because now you feel the need to spend more time at work. You have new work demands, and you have a lot to learn. You sometimes feel that you might not be capable of performing well in this new position.

Realizing that almost all change comes with positives and negatives, and lots of emotions to come along with all of those, might help us not to feel so alone and confused.

#3 - Life Doesn't Stop when You Reach Your Goals.

Can you remember the last time you reached an important goal? Did you even take any time to celebrate? Many of us rush right on to the next thing, then the next, without much of a pause to celebrate and realize that we just achieved something we've been working for. And often reaching a goal can feel more like relief than something to celebrate.

That's natural and normal - but it also can result in feeling like we're on an endless treadmill, going nowhere.

#4 - Success Doesn't Mean You'll Always be Happy

As you use this book to decide what success means to you personally, it might help to examine the experiences and emotions you expect to have if you are successful at getting what you want. How do you think your life will change? How do you think your feelings will change? You might be setting yourself up for disappointment, and you might be working toward the wrong thing.

Do you expect to always feel happy?

News flash - you'll still be you, with ALL your feelings. I believe that's a good thing, but if you expected to only feel happy, still having all your feelings can be a disappointment.

My Momtellectual interview with Natalie Merritt-Broderick illustrates the fact that even if you change things so you're living the life you want to live, the demons from your past can still follow you. Natalie spent many years in the corporate world trying to ignore her need for creativity - she left that version of "success" and is now an Inspirational Creative Artist. Natalie redefined success for herself - yet she still struggles with perfectionism. As an entrepreneurial artist, she also has to navigate creating things that are a true expression of herself while pleasing enough other people so she can make a living. (Overcoming Perfectionism and Judgement, Momtellectual Episode 145 - find it at tamsen.ca/momtellectual145).

#5 - Success Can't Fill You Up

When you're "successful" do you expect to feel WORTHY? Foreshadowing - you can't earn worthiness. We'll be talking about what to do instead in Curiosity #1 - Truth Bomb: You Can't Earn Self-Worth). It's totally ok and reasonable to want to have self-worth, to make that part of your version of success - but there are ways that work to get there, and ways that don't.

You need to figure out what you REALLY want.

I remember reading a story about a young man (let's call him Kyle) who grew up overweight. He had the horrible experience of growing up in a household where he was insulted and bullied for his weight, even by his own mother. He was desperate to feel loved. When he reached young adulthood, Kyle decided enough was enough, he was taking charge of his physical health and his body. He worked really hard, lost a lot of fat, gained muscle, and achieved his fitness goals.

Success! Kyle could be happy now.

But wait - he still didn't feel loved and accepted by his family, or people in general. He still felt inadequate and unworthy. So, Kyle decided that he could get love and approval by being involved in romantic relationships. Since he had done so much work on his body, he had little trouble finding women who would date him.

Success! Kyle could be happy now.

But wait - he STILL didn't feel loved and accepted, not really. What to do now? Maybe he just needed lots of sex to feel loved and worthy! He became fairly promiscuous.

Success?

As I remember it, Kyle ended up getting a sexually transmitted disease. That shook him up enough that he reevaluated his attempts to get love and approval through casual sexual relationships, since it not only wasn't working, but resulted in a serious health scare.

So, Kyle was successful in losing fat, gaining muscle, looking better, getting girlfriends, and being able to hook up with many women for casual sexual relationships. What he really wanted was to feel loved, so "succeeding" at something that he didn't want resulted in him feeling worse. Kyle couldn't feel loved just based on how other people treated him, he had a lot of internal work and healing to do, especially around being rejected as a child by his own family. He had to do that before he could even accept that he was loved by others.

You may want to improve some aspect of yourself, you may measure success by achieving or acquiring - a better body, a promotion, a baby, or a relationship. Those are great things to have, and to work for. But if you are trying to have those things because you don't feel worthy and think that you will magically somehow feel worthy after you reach those goals, it's my experience that you're wrong.

If you don't believe me and Jim Carrey, ask Matt Damon how he felt after winning an Oscar at 27 years old.

It can't fill you up. If there's a hole you have, that won't fill it. I felt so blessed to have that awareness at 27, at that age. Because I wouldn't have known it - unless I knew it. My heart broke for a second. I imagined another one of me, an old man, going 'Oh my God, where did my life go, what have I done?'

- Matt Damon

Five Growing Questions about Success:

1. Do any of the five reasons why success often sucks explored in chapter really seem to apply to your experience? Might it change how you define success? Here's the list:

    - Any change is a loss of the familiar

- Success can bring unexpected consequences
- Life doesn't stop when you reach your goals
- Success doesn't mean you'll always be happy
- Success can't fill you up

2. Who is someone you think of as very successful (it's fine to choose someone you know, or a famous person is fine too)? Why do you think they're successful? What is at least one thing you expect you would HATE about their life?

3. Do you think that success is something that you can achieve, or is it a never-ending quest?

4. Are you surprised by the included quotes about Jim Carrey and Matt Damon winning huge awards and it not being enough to convince them that they are "enough"? Does this change your perspective about pinning success and happiness on achieving recognition from others?

5. Is there something that you believe will help you feel successful but it goes against what you think most people see as successful? What are some barriers that you might face if you pursue this unaccepted version of success anyway?

Success Summary Question:

What was one thing you learned in this chapter about success that you want to include in your personal definition of success? Write or dictate a note for yourself, or put it in the appropriate section of the journal provided (find out how to download the journal for free at http://tamsen.ca/paradoxjournalfree).

> The best part is money, traveling, and the people you meet. The worst part is, again, money, travel, and the people you meet.
>
> - Carrie Fisher

Starting to Redefine Success

Define success on your own terms, achieve it by your own rules, and build a life you're proud to live.

- Anne Sweeney

This book is an invitation on a journey to FEELING truly successful. To do that, you need to decide what success means to you, personally.

We all get messages from our families, our friends, society, media - about what success looks like and what it "should" look like. Taking the time to evaluate those messages and figure out what success means to YOU can take some work.

The questions and information provided in this book will start you on your way.

As You Decide What Success Means for You, Consider 2 Things:

We'll be digging into these two points deeply in our final section while we're working to redefine success, but here's a preview:

1 - Make sure that what you call success depends on you and your actions, and not things you can't control - including other people. Focus on things you can control.

2 - Make sure that you can feel successful today, not 5 or 10 years or more in the future.

A good example of defining success in these 2 unhelpful ways comes from asking mothers what successful motherhood looks like. I've asked many mothers what it is to be a successful mother, and I often get comments that boil down to "When my child is a successful adult living according to my values, then I'll know I did a good job raising them."

Right.

First, 18 or more years is a LONG time to wait for feedback about whether you're doing a good job! Not much chance to change your strategies if they aren't working.

Second, any mom who has ever had their toddler throw themselves down on the grocery store floor screaming because you said no to the pastel marshmallow cereal knows that there's only so much control we really have over our kids.

If you want to feel like a successful mom, what are some pieces of the mothering puzzle that you do every day, or that you could work to improve on a daily basis, that could help you be (and feel) more successful? I try to spend at least 15 minutes playing and interacting with my son doing something fun. Right now, we often play Minecraft™, and so I work on also doing something that involves more eye contact!

What about you? What does being successful look like to you, and how could you DO that every day (or almost - remember to practice self-compassion as you go! We'll talk about the benefits of self-compassion in Curiosity #2 - The Paradox of Self-Compassion.

Five Growing Questions about Redefining Success:

1. What is an area of your life you'd like to be more successful in, and what does that look like to you, right now?

2. Look at your answer to #1 - what part of this is in your control?

3. Look at your answer to #2 - is there something there that you can do on a daily basis?

4. Create a statement about being successful that meets the criteria of being in your control and being something you can potentially do every day. Then, try doing more of whatever your success statement is! Be open to revising your personal success statement as we work through more challenges in this book.

5. As you incorporate the actions involved in your personal success statement from question #4, how does it feel? Check in with yourself about your progress. Do your best to take time to celebrate if you're successful daily, and practice self-compassion as you learn and grow!

Redefining Success Summary Question:

What was one thing you learned in this chapter about redefining success that you want to include in your personal definition of success? Write or dictate a note for yourself, or put it in the appropriate section of the journal provided (find out how to download the journal for free at http://tamsen.ca/paradoxjournalfree).

Everyone wants to live on top of the mountain, but all the happiness and growth occurs while you're climbing it.

- Andy Rooney

Section: Creating Self-Worth

Love yourself first and everything else falls into line. You really have to love yourself to get anything done in this world.

- Lucille Ball

Feeling "good enough" is part of success for many of us - even if we don't know it until we "arrive" and still DON'T feel good enough. I'm choosing to put working on your self-worth right up front for many reasons. Most of us have issues around this, so we could benefit from the work. As Lucille Ball says, loving ourselves seems to be fundamental to getting a lot of other stuff done - if something's holding you back, a lack of self-worth is a likely culprit. And hey - as we work on other areas of success, feeling good about ourselves makes life a heck of a lot more enjoyable!

Challenges that we often encounter when trying to feel more worthy that we'll discuss in this section include:

- How we often try to earn a feeling of self-worth - and why it fails.
- Why sometimes we "KNOW" we're worthy but struggle to actually FEEL it.
- The importance of practicing self-compassion when we struggle or mess up.
- Accepting that our emotions are an important and valuable part of us.
- Fighting the financial and power interests of people who make money from us feeling bad - especially about our bodies.

Self-Worth Orienting Questions:

1. Definition question: What does "self-worth" mean to you right now?
2. Self-assessment question: What is your current level of self-worth?

3. Goal question: What is the main thing you want to change about your self-worth?

4. Achievement question: How will you know you've achieved your self-worth goal?

We only become what we are by the radical and deep-seated refusal of that which others have made of us.

- Jean-Paul Sartre

Curiosity #1 - Truth Bomb: You Can't Earn Self-Worth

> You are imperfect, you are wired for struggle, but you are worthy of love and belonging.
>
> - Brené Brown

One of the key pieces of self-worth is knowing that we're worthy of being loved, and worthy of being accepted just as we are. Most of us want to feel like we belong. Brené Brown has done a lot of interesting and important research on that sense of belonging, and what disrupts it. She says that all her research shows only one difference between people who feel very connected and those who struggle for a sense of connection and belonging.

The only difference she's found is that the people who feel it KNOW THEY ARE WORTHY of love and connection.

Now this is an important thing to dive into, especially if you have the idea that somehow being worthy of love is something you have to earn. If the only difference between those that experience love and those that don't is a sense of self-worth, then how people are treated isn't the key factor. It's not that people who feel connected have earned a sense of worthiness - feeling worthy has to come first. The realization that you have to know you are worthy of love before you can truly feel loved is HUGE. Not already knowing that we're worthy of love is a key piece of why many of us struggle to feel loved.

> That's the Truth Bomb: We can't earn self-worth from someone else. **We need to know we're worthy before we can feel it**. Until we know we're worthy, how we're treated by other people will never be enough to prove to us we have worth.

Self-Worth - or Lack of it - is a Filter

Self-worth is like a filter - it's possible to be treated very well, but always find a way to see evidence that you're not worthy.

If you're out walking with your romantic partner, and they do a double take at an attractive person walking by, what would you think? Someone without a sense of self-worth might automatically start comparing themselves to the other person, feeling insecure and inadequate. They might suffer in silence, or start a fight by criticizing their partner for looking, or for any of a handful of other offences, real or imagined. Someone with self-worth might just shrug it off, or note that the person was wearing very colourful clothes that caught their partner's attention. They also might set a boundary that when you're walking with them, don't gawk at other people!

Knowing that you're worthy of love can't protect you from all bad relationships, from being rejected by a romantic partner, losing a job, or other disappointments in life. But having self-worth does insulate you from assuming that you got rejected because you're fundamentally flawed and unlovable.

We're Often Taught We're Not Worthy When We're Young

I struggled with a lack of self-worth from the earliest I can remember. One of the biggest reasons I know of is because my brother treated me really badly as we were growing up.

My brother John was 14 months younger than me, and pretty much my opposite. We were both smart, but I was a bookworm while he was athletic, I was painfully shy and awkward while he was popular, I was timid while he was a ringleader.

I was a rule follower while he was a rule breaker.

John and I had a really rough relationship, and his bullying started before we were teenagers. John was extremely cruel to me, emotionally and verbally. He would lunge for the wall and mash himself against it to avoid "contaminating" himself by touching me if we passed in the hallway. Stupid stuff like that, but it really hurt. Why was I so disgusting to my own brother?

The summer before I started at the University of Waterloo, John's risk taking caught up with him. He had a psychotic break as a reaction to some sort of street drug he took, and landed in the mental hospital. He was there for a few weeks. When he came home it was almost time for me to move to Waterloo, and in that short time there seemed to be a bit of an uneasy truce between us. The truce seemed to last through my first few weekend visits home. It was a relief, but also weird.

Then, in mid November, John took the family Camaro and drove it at high speed into the side of a bridge. While he succeeded in destroying the car, he didn't quite succeed at dying - that time. John was severely physically injured including sustaining severe brain damage. He spent several months in a coma. I'm sure you can imagine how wonderful Christmas was that year for my family.

I'm not going to spend a lot of time talking about suicide in this book, but for those of us who have experienced family members or friends dying by suicide, often we're discouraged from talking about it. If you'd like to hear a bit more about my experience around my brother's suicide, hear Elaine Turcotte's story about her experience with suicide in her family, and understand how sharing the pain we feel from being close to someone who dies by suicide and other traumas can help us connect with others and heal, you can check out Momtellectual episode 48, We Need to Talk about Suicide (you can find it at tamsen.ca/momtellectual48).

John slowly started to come out of his coma, very slowly started to seem aware of his surroundings, and gradually relearned to talk, walk, eat, all that stuff most of us take for granted. I remember on his first visits home my mom would take down the fake plant hanging in the corner and sit my brother under the hook and use it to hang his food bag after attaching it to the peg coming out of his stomach.

At one point during all this, it really hit me how brain damaged he was, and it seemed as though the person he had been was basically gone. I decided to start over - at one point he could accept hugs, and he hugged my mom and dad, and I asked if I could hug him too. He nodded, and we hugged, and I let his previous cruelty be something that belonged to someone else who was gone. It didn't make the situation easy - it was hard to be around him and to watch my parents struggle with how to help him and with their own grief - but at least the cruelty was gone.

But only for awhile.

Two summers later he was back living with my parents, going back to high school, and able to walk with a cane. He was scheduled for eye surgery the next week, and I was just about to leave from a visit home to go back to university. I was upstairs and went to say goodbye to him - he whispered that he had a secret to tell me, and I wasn't to tell our parents.

I agreed to keep what John was going to tell me a secret. I honestly thought he was about to tell me that he was afraid of the surgery, but didn't want to worry our parents by telling them. I shake my head at my total misread of the situation now, but I thought he was about to confide in me. He then told me - in a more profanity laced speech - that "Our parents hate you - you failed school, you're a loser, go away and never come back.

Never ever come back here. I don't want to see you, Mom and Dad hate you. They want you to get lost. Leave."

I was so taken by surprise at this cruelty, appearing to me to be out of the blue - I tried to persuade him that he was wrong - I knew our parents didn't hate me, even though I had failed several courses the last term. The abuse continued. "They DO hate you! Leave! Don't come back! F—k off!"

One decision that I made was to keep my word not to tell our parents. Not for him, but because they were dealing with enough. Numb, I went downstairs, finished packing up my car, and somehow said goodbye to my parents without them cluing in that something was horribly wrong. I got in my car, and drove part way around the circular driveway, until the cedar hedge hid me from the house.

And then I sat in the car bawling my eyes out for what felt like a very very long time.

Being Rejected Causes Shame

I felt angry, betrayed, sad, disappointed, extremely hurt. I also felt a lot of shame. John had verbally kicked me hard where it hurt. I felt very disappointed in myself for my poor performance at school. I was in chemistry at that time, and chemistry had turned into physics which had turned into calculus. Calculus and I have never been friends. Calculus kicked my butt all around the campus and back again. I knew my parents loved me, even though I had failed most of my courses. I also knew I had disappointed them, and it sucked.

I felt shame because I felt stupid for trusting John, and letting him emotionally close enough to hurt me like this again. Why hadn't I known better? I was an idiot. And I also felt shame because this was my BROTHER. He was FAMILY. Family is supposed to love you, to care about you just as you are, to be on your side. Family is NOT supposed to tell you to f—k off, to go away and never come back, and to glory in causing you pain.

What was so wrong with me that a member of my own family couldn't even tolerate me?

We All Deserve Love

In listening to that shame, that pain and confusion about why John despised me, the burning in my eyes, churning in my stomach, the tears, I started to hear something else. Something from deep inside, my spirit, my heart, my guts.

No one deserves to be treated like this.

No one.

No. One. Ever.

I live in the grey zones, I allow for uncertainty. I sometimes joke that I won't even say I 100% believe the sun will come up in the morning. But in that moment I knew with a blazing, white-hot certainty that the treatment I had just received was not something that I deserved. If no one deserves it, then even I didn't, even if my self respect was in the toilet. I decided that I didn't have to take his treatment as a true statement about my value.

I was done.

You've probably heard it put this way: How people treat us says way more about THEM than it does about US. It seems like common sense to me now, but it was an earth-shattering revelation at the time. Now, when someone rejects me, it hurts, but I don't have to believe it says anything about who I am or what I'm worth. If you're ready to learn and reinforce such things, now is your time to challenge those things that are holding you back.

Ask yourself these questions about self-worth. Be open to the idea that knowing you're worthy needs to come before you can experience it. When you're done answering the growing questions, consider what you would like to bring from this chapter into your personal definition of success.

Five Growing Questions about Self-Worth:

1. What were you taught growing up about when you were worthy of love, and when you were not?

2. What do you believe NOW about what makes a person valuable and worthy of love?

3. If your answer to #2 was anything other than simply being human, would shifting your belief about what makes someone worthy of love be helpful for you?

4. How would your life be different if you had rock solid self-worth? How would it stay the same?

5. Do you agree that someone who treats you badly is someone you can choose to avoid, yet still see them as human and worthy of love? Why or why not?

Self-Worth Summary Question:

What was one thing you learned in this chapter about self-worth that you want to include in your personal definition of success? Write or dictate a note for yourself, or put it in the appropriate section of the journal provided (find out how to download the journal for free at http://tamsen.ca/paradoxjournalfree).

Don't rely on someone else for your happiness and self-worth. Only you can be responsible for that. If you can't love and respect yourself - no one else will be able to make that happen. Accept who you are - completely; the good and the bad - and make changes as YOU see fit - not because you think someone else wants you to be different.

- Stacey Charter

Curiosity #2 - The Paradox of Self-Compassion

One of the best guides to how to be self-loving is to give ourselves the love we are often dreaming about receiving from others.

- Bell Hooks

Have you ever been challenged to really listen when you talk to yourself?

What do you say to yourself when you're feeling sad or disappointed?

What do you say to yourself when you make a mistake?

What do you say to yourself when you're afraid?

Think about how you talk to yourself, and then consider asking yourself - would you ever EVER consider saying those things to another human being?! It's really hard to nurture a sense of self-worth - and to feel successful - if we're talking to ourselves like we're crazy, evil, or stupid when things aren't perfect.

What is Self-Compassion?

Sometimes it's difficult to get a handle on exactly what self-compassion is. Self-compassion isn't about telling ourselves that we're amazing whatever we do. Sometimes we do make mistakes, and everyone has room to grow.

I really find clarity in how to treat myself with compassion when I consider myself as a true friend, and what I would say to other friends. If a good friend messes up, I wouldn't tell them that it doesn't matter. Especially if they're busy telling me how horrible they feel! In most cases, I would listen, and make sure that they knew I loved and accepted them despite their mistake. When they were ready, I would help them work through how to make it better, or how to do better next time. More information about how to emotionally support friends so they FEEL supported is the focus of Curiosity #8 - The Paradox of Support.

We'll be talking about what it means to be a real friend in Curiosity #9 - Truth Bomb: You Need to be the Friend You Want, and expanding that discussion to what it means to be a real friend to ourselves. But this chapter is about connecting and creating a healthy relationship with ourselves, and self-compassion deserves a whole chapter!

Beating Yourself up Causes a lot of Harm

The time that I can remember being hardest on myself was a few months after my son was born. After 3 years of fertility treatments and three miscarriages, I finally had my son. He was demanding (as is normal for babies!) and I made it through the first 4 months emotionally ok even though I was exhausted.

I talked about this in the Paradox of Success chapter, yet it's worth mentioning that about 4 months after my son was born I started getting really anxious and had trouble sleeping even though I was totally exhausted (hello, postpartum depression!) I started beating myself up for not feeling happy and grateful all the time since I finally had my son. I really can't know how much worse I made my depression, but I do think that feeling bad for feeling bad was certainly not at all helpful!

I now know that becoming a mom was a huge change for me, which was a grief experience. My life totally changed and although I was very grateful for my son and love him very much, that didn't mean that I had to be ok with not having time to shower or being exhausted all the time.

I deserved to give myself a break!

I would have had a lot more energy and been able to not only be a better mom but enjoy myself more if I had practiced more self-compassion.

Self-Compassion Helps Us Persevere

It might seem that practicing self-compassion is "letting yourself off the hook." But maybe self-compassion is more about not beating yourself up for something you already feel horrible about, and giving yourself the freedom to try to make it right and move on without inflicting too much additional damage.

Evidence suggests that self-compassion is a tool that helps us do more, and generally be more peaceful in our lives. Researchers Kristin Neff and Christopher Germer are experts in "mindful self-compassion", and they have found many beneficial effects (if you'd like more information, check out the Resources section at the back of this book). Practicing self-compassion is related to persistence - the ability to continue trying in the face of setbacks. Treating yourself with kindness when you do suffer a setback lets you bounce back more quickly, and avoid spending tons of time and mental energy on beating yourself up. If we're too afraid of making mistakes to try, that will discourage us when things get hard.

It makes just as much sense that letting yourself off the hook for mistakes would result in you being willing to do more and be more, rather than just being motivation to sit on the couch.

> That's the paradox of self-compassion - being more accepting of our mistakes and treating ourselves with kindness - instead of increasing our mistakes and failures by "letting us off the hook", **self-compassion tends to increase our sense of self-worth, improve our performance, and increase our willingness to persevere when we're challenged.**

Most of us have had the experience of getting into a spiral of negative thinking. Maybe someone said something at work and you don't know how to interpret it, but it probably isn't good. Maybe you went on a date with someone, and they aren't returning your calls. Maybe you don't like how you look, or how your neighbour looked at you. Whatever it is, you can probably relate to the feeling like you have a whole bunch of energy wrapped up in that situation. It's energy that you don't feel like you're giving voluntarily, and it's unavailable for other things. You feel tired, and drained, and there's an undercurrent of annoyance in daily activities because you just can't free yourself from this thing that's hanging over you.

That is one place where self-compassion can help, although practicing self-compassion can be tough.

Practicing Self-Compassion

So how do you practice self-compassion? Practice is an important word - it does take practice for most of us. And also patience, and self-compassion as we learn self-compassion!

Can you just let yourself be, without judging, even though your thoughts race and you don't feel you can control them? Can you let that be ok, even if just for a little while?

Can it be ok that you care what someone else thinks of you, even though we get told over and over that we shouldn't let it bother us?

Can you practice thinking of yourself as a good friend, and treat yourself accordingly?

Practice. It's worth it.

Five Growing Questions about Self-Compassion:

1. Pay attention to how you talk to yourself when things don't go your way or you make a mistake. How compassionate are you to yourself?

2. What is one thing you could change to be better friends with yourself?

3. When is the last time you remember someone showing you compassion? What did they say and do? What did it feel like?

4. Think of a time someone else made a mistake and you wanted to help them feel better about it. What did you do? What did you say?

5. Next time you make a mistake, go back to #4. Do the same things for yourself you did for someone else. Pay close attention to how it feels. It may feel really good, or it may not. Practice self-compassion either way. What did you learn from this?

Self-Compassion Summary Question:

What was one thing you learned in this chapter about self-compassion that you want to include in your personal definition of success? Write or dictate a note for yourself, or put it in the appropriate section of the journal provided (find out how to download the journal for free at http://tamsen.ca/paradoxjournalfree).

I found in my research that the biggest reason people aren't more self-compassionate is that they are afraid they'll become self-indulgent. They believe self-criticism is what keeps them in line. Most people have gotten it wrong because our culture says being hard on yourself is the way to be.

- Kristen Neff

Curiosity #3 - The Happiness Myth

The way I see it, if you want the rainbow, you gotta put up with the rain!

- Dolly Parton

It should be easier to feel whole than to feel broken. So why isn't it so?

It's shockingly simple.

From almost the moment we're born, we're taught to numb and hide our emotions.

"Big kids don't cry."

"You're sad? Here's a cookie!"

"Go to your room until you can come out with a smile on your face!"

Trying to feel successful and well with these emotional "tools" is like trying to feel whole by cutting off your arm with a chainsaw.

It's truly a vicious cycle. Most of us don't know how to deal with painful emotions - our own or other people's. That makes painful feelings VERY scary and something to be avoided. So we minimize them, criticize them, hide them, numb them - and we assume that others should do the same.

We don't know how to help others heal from painful feelings - so we either run from other people when they have painful feelings, or try to get them to not feel. If you can relate to this, I hope that it's a relief that there ARE ways to heal from painful emotions, and you can learn them - and teach them too.

Without cookies. Or cupcakes. Though there is definitely a place for cupcakes!

Does Eliminating Pain Increase Happiness?

I call it the "mathematical model" of happiness. To foreshadow - it's totally wrong.

There's this idea that a lot of us have that to be happy, we need to add things into our life that "make" us happy, and subtract the things that cause us emotional pain. Often, we try to erase the painful emotions themselves. So it goes something like this - for more happiness, add more happy, and subtract sadness, fear, anger, and anything else "bad".

The expected equation is + happy - pain = HAPPY!!!!

Logical, right? But we're dealing with emotions, which are an entirely different type of information and don't always follow logical rules. The actual result? Usually less happy and more of the painful feelings that we tried to squash, or a feeling of emotional numbness.

> That's the happiness myth - getting rid of your pain doesn't make you happier. Instead, **numbing your pain means killing your joy.**

Is Happiness the ANSWER?

Likely as part of your success journey you want - expect - to feel happier. We often talk about success as "I'll be happy when..."

Our society puts a lot of stock in being happy. Our society also treats painful emotions as evil, as sick, as something to be avoided at all costs. Grief and sadness are things that we should "get over" or "rise above", very, very quickly. If your parent, spouse, or child dies, you're allowed to take a few days off work, and then you're expected to be back, acting "normally". If you're still sad after a month, and open about it? People wonder why you're still sad - and you're a candidate to be treated for a mental illness like depression.

Treating grieving people as sick? Now THAT is crazy.

I think part of this is just that painful emotions - they're PAINFUL! Our society doesn't deal well with discomfort, and so we're taught to avoid it. There's also a lot of money being made on things that are designed to distract us, to keep us occupied, to feed our addictions.

I also think part of this is confusion, which can lead to fear, which then also leads to avoidance. We're confused because we aren't taught what to DO. We just don't know what to do to help someone who is in emotional pain. We'll be covering that in Curiosity #8 - The Paradox of Support. We also don't know what to ask for when we're hurting. This fear leads to a general attempt to shut down, run from, distract ourselves from our feelings.

There are at least 5 things that can happen when we try to avoid painful feelings. All of these 5 things lead to less happiness, and it being harder to feel successful.

#1 - If We Numb Pain, We Numb Everything

First, if we numb any of our feelings, we numb everything. Brené Brown says her research shows that you can't selectively numb feelings. So, running away, distracting ourselves, or otherwise numbing ourselves to emotional pain means we numb our happy too.

Being numb is a pretty crappy way to go through life. It can take some rethinking to accept that we need to be open to the rain if we want the rainbow like Dolly Parton says, but it's true.

#2 - Numbing Our Feelings Cuts off an Important Information Source

Second, if we numb or otherwise avoid our feelings, we lose a very valuable source of information. Our emotions evolved to help us STAY ALIVE. Our different painful emotions have different messages, and it's important to pay attention to what we need to do to heal and stay safe.

Dismissing emotional information is something we're encouraged to do, with the idea that thinking and logic are more valuable. But emotional information is hugely valuable, it's just different!

#3 - Cutting Off Our Feelings Cuts Off Part of Who We Are

Third, when we cut off our emotions, we're cutting ourselves off from something that is a key part of who we are. We lose touch with a vital part of ourselves. It's like trying to feel healthy while chopping off bits of your body (parts you need - I'm not talking about trimming your nails or getting a haircut!)

Trying to ignore that emotion is an important part of yourself can lead to problems with self-worth in addition to emotional problems.

#4 - Cutting Off Pain Means Cutting Off Empathy

Fourth, cutting off pain means cutting off empathy, and the ability to truly connect with others. One of the most bonding experiences possible is supporting someone or being supported by them during an emotionally painful experience. Empathy means we're willing to feel what others feel, and that means feel some of their pain.

Being willing to take on a bit of someone's pain, to have their pain call to your own heart, can be a truly wonderful, bonding, and healing experience. Yes, it seems contradictory that pain is healing. But think about when you exercise your muscles - as they get stronger, it often hurts. Sharing pain can help grow a relationship in a similar way.

#5 - Joy Leads to Fear

Fifth, we run into the JOY = FEAR thing. This is another piece of Brené Brown wisdom (if you didn't know already, yes, I'm a fan).

It took me awhile to get it when I read Dr. Brown's statement that joy is the scariest of all emotions for many people. And then that night I was lying in bed next to my sleeping son, smelling his hair, feeling full of love, wonder and joy at this amazing human I get to have as part of my family. Enjoying the moment of being close to him, hugging him, feeling him breathe.

And then the fear hit.

He could stop breathing. I could lose him. He could die. He could get hit by a bus, get some dread disease. Could I possibly accidentally suffocate him in his sleep!?!

Aha! Joy = FEAR!!

I let myself feel it, this horrible fear of loss. It was painful and very scary. But letting myself feel it - it did go away. It took a minute or two, which felt like a lot longer - but it did go.

This may sound strange - but just like I feared the loss of my son, we can suffer from losses that haven't happened. It's anticipatory grief - we suffer not only when we experience losses, but our wonderful human way of being also lets us anticipate losses. When we have something great? We get to imagine what our experience will be like when we no longer have it.

Even when we get to experience happiness, it can quickly get ripped from us by pain.

So What on Earth to Do?

Realize that to feel like a complete person, emotionally whole, you need to eventually be able to feel all your feelings, and respect them for what they are. The first step is just feeling what you feel, without judgement. Feel your feelings without criticizing yourself for not being happy, and not trying to logic your way out of something you might be uncomfortable feeling.

I think we should consider changing our story about happiness. Happiness is just a feeling, a mood, happiness is intended to come and go. It's a wonderful thing to experience - but it's only part of a whole life, of living fully. What about if we use emotional wholeness for our goal, as a feeling of success, instead? That means that the whole of our emotions are important, that we as a whole are important. Let's get rid of the gaping hole left by our rejection of part of ourselves. We can't feel more whole by cutting off our feelings.

Before we head into the Five Growing Questions, this is a place where I think you might benefit from me providing some additional resources to support you in a journey toward emotional health.

More Resources for Emotional Health

If you're struggling with your emotional health yet you don't know where to start to feel better, you're far from alone. Here are some additional resources that can help you get started.

- Brené Brown. Seriously. Check out her stuff - she is an awesome researcher storyteller who focuses on the importance of emotions, love, and belonging. She has a couple of amazing TED talks and books, a blog, lots of amazing stuff.

- The Grief Recovery Method Handbook is also another great place to get more information. Grief is a reaction to any change, and it is not one emotion, but is an emotional experience that can encompass any and all emotions. I highly recommend learning about how to be emotionally safe and healthy, and this is a great system to use. They also have a website with a lot of blog posts that are great resources.

- For an exploration of what each individual emotion and emotional experience might be trying to tell you, check out "The Language of Emotions: What Your Feelings Are Trying to Tell You" by Karla McLauren. I don't necessarily agree with everything she says, but her book is really interesting and provoked me to lots of thinking.

Five Growing Questions about Happiness:

1. Do you need to include happiness in your definition of success? Why or why not?

2. How do you feel about changing the goal of being happy to the goal of being emotionally well?

3. How comfortable are you with your own painful feelings like sadness, anger, and fear?

4. How were you raised to treat painful feelings?

5. When someone cries in front of you, how do you feel? What would it take for you to just sit with them, let them cry, and stay present?

Happiness Summary Question:

What was one thing you learned in this chapter about happiness that you want to include in your personal definition of success? Write or dictate a note for yourself, or put it in the appropriate section of the journal provided (find out how to download the journal for free at http://tamsen.ca/paradoxjournalfree).

> We cannot selectively numb emotion. If we numb the dark, we numb the light. If we take the edge off pain and discomfort, we are, by default, taking the edge off joy, love, belonging, and the other emotions that give meaning to our lives.
>
> - Brené Brown

Curiosity #4 - The Confidence Myth

Stay afraid, but do it anyway. What's important is the action. You don't have to wait to be confident. Just do it and eventually the confidence will follow.

- Carrie Fisher

When I talk about confidence, the definition I use is having a sense of trust and safety. Confidence is a lack of fear and anxiety. One type of confidence is confidence in your ability. Part of what many people either explicitly want from success, or assume that success will bring them, is a feeling of confidence and trust in their abilities.

Unfortunately, many people get the order of feeling confident in their ability to do something and the actual doing backwards.

Confidence in Ability Takes Practice

I can think back to when I was learning to drive - I was terrified. I didn't want to learn. My mom had to force me to take my driving lessons. We lived out in the country, and she was tired of having to drive me everywhere!

I remember the instructor having me drive... Veeeeery slowly... Around an empty parking lot. I was very aware that I had control over a big huge piece of metal that could go really fast, and people could get hurt. Including me! I'm a confident driver now, after over 30 years of practice.

That's one thing about having confidence in our ability - we shouldn't expect to have confidence when we're really new at something! We need practice first. But how many times have you heard someone say (or even felt yourself) that you wanted to be more confident BEFORE you tried something? We need a bit of a perspective shift, and to be willing to be a little uncomfortable. That's part of the path to confidence.

> That's the Confidence Myth - we hesitate to try something new because we want to feel confident we will be successful BEFORE we try - **but confidence usually comes AFTER practice.**

I was in a waiting room a few years ago when a toddler was making his way down a hallway. He was… Toddling, for the most part. It was absolutely adorable to watch, because he was SO happy to be walking! He would stand up, raise his arms up in a victory pose, and take a few steps, screaming in joy.

Then he'd fall. Again and again.

His curly hair would wobble ferociously as he'd struggle up, strike his victory pose, let out another shriek with this huge, amazing grin, and take a few more steps. Obviously, he wasn't a hugely successful walker yet. But, he wasn't afraid of falling, or of failing.

Toddlers persist in learning to walk mostly because it's a developmental stage. They don't likely consider the pros and cons of what will happen - they just do. It's later on in life when we struggle so fiercely to feel safe and in control, even when trying new things. We create these nightmare scenarios in our head about how badly things will turn out, and we let that stop us from even starting.

In discussing confidence in ability with my friend Rachel a few years ago, she helped me see that confidence in ability needs to be divided into 2 types of confidence. There's confidence that you know what you need to know to do something, and then there's the confidence you get from practice and actively getting better at doing the thing. Knowing versus doing.

The Learning Trap

Entrepreneurs are a curious bunch. As a whole, we're pretty courageous, in terms of being willing to try new things and being able to deal with uncertainty. Yet there's something holding most of us back - and for many entrepreneurs I know, it usually comes down to sales and marketing. For some awesome entrepreneurs I know, it's partially that they're introverted, and so they really don't like things like networking events and find it tough to spend a lot of time interacting with other people. For me, I love people, so that's not it.

Rachel also helped me realize that one of the traps I fall into is going back into learning when I feel uncomfortable doing. Where I feel intimidated is the marketing and selling piece. Like many other entrepreneurs, I shudder at the idea of coming across as the stereotypical slimy, selfish salesperson only interested in people as mobile wallets. I love learning and getting more information - so learning is my safe place. That means when I don't feel confident in my ability, I head back to learning - and away from doing.

Sometimes, I legitimately need to learn more. I was following various "sales" gurus and some of their values just didn't mesh with mine. So, I found a few people with great ideas and successful businesses that fit in with my values, and that did help a lot.

But I still had to get out and DO more before I could really feel fully confident in my ability.

Focus on Practice

No matter how much you read about how to ride a bicycle, or how many videos you watch, or how often you go to the park and watch other people wheel around, that doesn't get you much better at doing it.

Sometimes we need to get used to failing. To hearing "no", or to falling off the bike, and realizing that we're still alive. We may be bruised, but we'll heal, and if we want to accomplish something then it's worth it. Sometimes rejection is our greatest fear. Curiosity #10 - The Paradox of Loneliness will cover why we're afraid of rejection and what to do about it.

Sometimes we just need to start out slow, and build up to where we want to be. It can be frustrating that this takes time (I think Malcolm Gladwell says 10,000 hours, but that's depressing).

We have a saying in our house, whenever anyone makes a mistake. "Who makes mistakes? Everyone." It's helping us get our son to try new things, but it's also an important reminder to all of us that mistakes are a part of life.

Get a Mentor

A very effective way to help you build confidence in your ability is to find a great mentor.

I remember being REALLY terrified of teaching when I started graduate school. I would spend most of the week preparing to teach, panicked. I was absolutely horrified by the idea not only of being stared at by a bunch of students, but also - what if I looked stupid? What if I couldn't answer a question?

I had an excellent mentor, Professor Albert Katz. I remember him explaining to me that there was nothing wrong with not being able to answer a question - and he taught me how to handle it. He said - never dismiss a question as unimportant. Acknowledge if you can't answer it, and let the class know that you'll look into it, and have an answer at the next class. And then DO IT. That's how you keep the respect of the class even when you don't know everything - and no one knows everything. If you're struggling to feel confident, it can help a lot to hear from someone with more experience, both about what typical challenges are, and how to overcome them.

If you'd like to dig deeper into my view of confidence and how to have more of it, you can check out my Tamsen Connects resource page at https://www.tamsenconnects.com/resources, or get free weekly tips by signing up at tamsen.ca/confidencetips.

Five Growing Questions about Confidence:

1. Do you try to feel confident before you try something new? Are you willing to make mistakes and get practice instead? How does this feel?

2. Are you procrastinating about something? Do you think it's related to a lack of confidence in your ability?

3. Have you had a mentor? How did they help?

4. Could you be a mentor to someone in your life? What's the best piece of advice you could give? What difference might it have made had you learned that piece of advice earlier?

5. Do you fall into the trap of trying to learn more when you need practice instead?

Confidence Summary Question:

What was one thing you learned in this chapter about confidence that you want to include in your personal definition of success? Write or dictate a note for yourself, or put it in the appropriate section of the journal provided (find out how to download the journal for free at http://tamsen.ca/paradoxjournalfree).

If you want to learn to swim jump into the water. On dry land no frame of mind is ever going to help you.

- Bruce Lee

Curiosity #5 - Truth Bomb: Stop Dieting

"You are not broken. The 'eat less, then sleep less so you can exercise more' approach is broken."

- Jonathan Bailor

How do you feel about your body?

Most women I talk to HATE at least some aspect of their body, and it's important to address that on our journey to real success. Our bodies are a fundamental piece of US. Our body is the most basic tool for interacting with the world, with our loved ones. We need our body to hug!

Here's an important thing to think about: Have you noticed that there are a lot of people making a lot of money because people feel fat and hate their bodies? People are selling diet plans and diet "food", protein shakes, nutritional supplements, calorie tracking apps - and of course the surgical interventions!

Lots of money changes hands.

I'll be bold enough to say that many of the companies making and selling these "solutions" know their customers will fail long term in attempts to reshape their body - and are literally banking on it.

What does the Science Say?

If you want a really good review of the science around fitness and nutrition, look up Jonathan Bailor's The Calorie Myth - it's available as a book, as a CreativeLIVE course, and you can find lots about it on the web.

It's definitely dense with research, so I'll briefly summarize his findings.

The traditional "eat less and exercise more" approach to losing weight and getting healthy fails for about 95% of us - and scientific data has shown that for decades.

> That's the Truth Bomb: Traditional diets and exercise don't work for most people who want to lose weight or be more physically healthy. **What you eat is far more important than how much you eat.**

One of the best things I like about Bailor's approach is that he's open about the fact that not every eating plan will work for everyone - and to try things and do what works for you. If you're one of the 5% or so who are succeeding at the "eat less exercise more" plan, then go for it - but if you're not, changing what you eat - not the amount - is most likely to be helpful.

Check out Bailor's work if you'd like to see what he recommends we eat, and what to avoid.

Stop Counting Calories

If you want to lose weight or feel better, I strongly suggest you stop the calorie reduction kind of dieting. Even "success" at following a plan to reduce calories usually results in you feeling really horrible, and personally I don't call that success. Annoyingly, this kind of diet also tends to cause you to be less healthy and gain even more weight in the long term.

Make your own decision - again, if calorie counting is working for you and you do feel successful, go for it. But if it's not, stop doing things that don't work. Also consider that if you're unhappy about how you look, you might need to do more mental and emotional work than physical work.

Food and Emotion

Let's address the fact that many of us have been taught to deal with painful emotions with food.

You feel bad? Hey - have a cookie! You'll feel better.

We need food to survive. Food isn't something we can just avoid - yet for many of us deciding what to eat feels like a minefield, or a pop quiz! Eating food - especially unhealthy food - can be a hugely unhelpful behaviour and decrease our quality of life in the long run. But eating "bad" food feels GOOD right now! And if we don't have other effective methods for dealing with painful feelings, then we'll tend to bring on the brownies.

Hey - I'm not overall dissing brownies. And cake… Mmmmm… Chocolate cake, with chocolate icing… Let me drown in drool over here for awhile. But…

Enjoying a Treat is Different than Numbing Your Feelings with Food

Maybe you haven't considered this before - but eating a brownie because you enjoy it is different than eating a brownie because you want to numb your feelings. And unfortunately, if you're eating a brownie to avoid your feelings, you're unlikely to stop at one.

One good clue about whether you're using food to shift your emotions is whether you can defy that old potato chip commercial and eat just one. Sometimes one - or two, or a handful - is all you need to feel satisfied. I'll admit that eating one potato chip and being done would be rare. But eating one or two handfuls? Sure, if you have several handfuls and still aren't satisfied, maybe you've let yourself get too hungry for a meal, and you should eat dinner instead. I know I do this when I'm not careful! Yet if you've had dinner and you finish a large package of chips and are still looking for more, you might need more than potato chips. Sometimes we've just let ourselves get too hungry, but sometimes we're trying to use food as a numbing agent or a distraction.

I think it's telling that research indicates many - maybe most - people in North America associate chocolate cake with guilt. We KNOW that certain foods aren't good for us - but we eat them anyway. And you know what? I'm not going to say do away with all the foods you love! I personally believe that eating shouldn't be reduced to an unenjoyable, strictly utilitarian process. That's not my point.

My suggestion is...

Become Aware of When You are Using Food to Change Your Feelings.

If you become aware that you do use food to deal with painful feelings, finding more effective ways to process and heal those painful feelings might be the main work you need to do if you want to change what you eat and how your body looks.

Yet awareness is only the first step. If you want to understand how to increase your joy, you can review Curiosity #3 - The Happiness Myth, and if you need healthy emotional support, we'll be covering that in Curiosity #8 - The Paradox of Support. Self-compassion can be key here! Review Curiosity #2 - The Paradox of Self-Compassion if you need to - as often as you need to.

And here's a Momtellectual Podcast episode for you if you're feeling shame around eating. M.B. Sherrin is a registered psychologist who was working to help obese patients - and found that although she's not obese, she deeply related to her patients' disordered eating. In our interview, M.B. was open about the shame she felt over her eating behaviour, and the feeling like she should have been able to figure out that she had problems way before she did. As part of her own healing, she created a Not for Profit called MetaShift, and a program called My Hungry Head to help people understand and heal their unhealthy thoughts around food and eating (My Hungry Head, Momtellectual episode 108. You can find it at tamsen.ca/momtellectual108).

Unrealistic Standards Make People a Lot of Money - and Leave Most of Us Feeling Ugly

I would love to say that we can change the world, and that we should all jump on the "body positivity" bandwagon. I do believe this - but we have to do it in the context of people still making HUGE amounts of money when they feed on our feelings of inadequacy. That means when we work to understand that we are amazing exactly as we are right now, we're going to face pushback from people and organizations that make money from us feeling horrible about ourselves.

Companies and influencers who work to maintain unrealistic standards are one example of this. Even supermodels have been quoted as not recognizing their bodies when they see them on the cover of magazines - even the most beautiful people in the world are usually airbrushed and otherwise altered beyond recognition. I feel it's an important act of rebellion to work on accepting ourselves as we are right now, including physically. It's not only a kind of success that we can achieve, it's an act of rebellion against the industries that profit from feeding our inadequacies.

Here are some questions to get you started:

Five Growing Questions about Dieting:

1. How do you feel about how your body looks? What would you like it to look like instead? Do you think this is a realistic goal?

2. Do you use food to change your feelings? How often?

3. How much guilt do you feel about food? How do you think your eating habits would change if the guilt just disappeared?

4. Check your media use - social media accounts you follow, magazines you read, television programs you watch, etc. Do you see images that reinforce realistic or unrealistic bodies?

5. Remember your body of 10 years ago. Would you like to have it back? How did you feel about it then?

Dieting Summary Question:

What was one thing you learned in this chapter about dieting that you want to include in your personal definition of success? Write or dictate a note for yourself, or put it in the appropriate section of the journal provided (find out how to download the journal for free at http://tamsen.ca/paradoxjournalfree).

Food is an important part of a balanced diet.

- Fran Lebowitz

Creating Self-Worth: Summary

You yourself, as much as anybody in the entire universe, deserve your love and affection.

- Buddha

The Self-Worth section is about creating and maintaining a healthy connection with your true self. In this summary section, we're checking back in to see what's changed with the new insights you have gained, and what feels most important to you.

You may be able to answer these questions right away. You may also want to re-examine your answers to the review questions from each chapter in this section, and decide on which feels the most important to include in your personal definition of success right now.

Remember that there is no "right" or "wrong" answer. If you're having trouble deciding, don't stress about it. There will be time to decide what to focus on when you're deciding on your action plan - and I'll introduce some strategies to help you deal with overwhelm if you're still having trouble deciding then!

Self-Worth Review Questions:

Check in - has reading this section and answering the questions changed any of your answers?

1. Definition review question: What does "self-worth" mean to you right now, after reading this section?

2. Self-assessment review question: What is your current level of self-worth after reading this section?

3. Goal review question: What is the main thing you want to change about your self-worth, after reading this section?

4. Achievement review question: How will you know you've achieved your self-worth goal?

Don't try to prove anything about yourself to anyone. It isn't necessary. Your worth shines through to others. Know your worth.

- Alexandra Stoddard

Section: Creating Healthy Relationships

"It is necessary, and even vital, to set standards for your life and the people you allow in it."

- Mandy Hale

Relationships are important to many of us - yet when most people talk about success, relationships aren't usually the first thing we mention. And if we do, it's often romantic relationships and not our friendships that we include in our definition of success.

BIG mistake.

There is evidence that the quality of our social connections has a huge impact on our quality of life - and even that lack of positive social connections can be more dangerous to our physical health than smoking and obesity. If you're interested in digging deep into the effects of loneliness, I highly recommend

John Cacioppo and William Patrick's book Loneliness: Human Nature and the Need for Social Connection.

In this section we're going to examine several things about relationships and how we see them so that we can include healthy relationships explicitly in our definition of success. We'll talk about why "just don't care what other people think" is unrealistic - and unhelpful - advice. We'll examine what makes someone a good friend, and the importance of YOU focusing on being a good friend, to yourself and others. We'll ask ourselves questions about what a soul mate is, and whether they even exist.

We'll also ask very important questions about emotional support, including what healthy emotional support is and how to give it (and how to ask for it when you need it!)

The health of our relationships is also an important part of whether we experience feeling worthy. As we discussed in the Creating Self-Worth section, we need to KNOW we're worthy before we can experience it. But we also need to experience being treated as worthy before we can truly FEEL it - and being treated badly can erode our sense of self-worth.

Healthy Relationships Orienting questions:

1. Definition question: What does "healthy relationship" mean to you right now?

2. Self-assessment question: How healthy are your relationships right now?

3. Goal question: What is the main thing you want to change about the health of your relationships?

4. Achievement question: How will you know you've achieved your relationship health goal?

To know oneself is to study oneself in action with another person.

- Bruce Lee

Curiosity #6 - The Paradox of Independence

People who say they don't care what people think are usually desperate to have people think they don't care what people think.

- George Carlin

I met Ashley at a networking meeting a few years ago, and we arranged to have a coffee to get to know each other better. She's a photographer, a writer, and a coach, but what shines through everything is her love of stories. She is amazing not only at telling stories, but helping others find THEIR stories. Ashley glows as she talks about inspiring others to tell their most true and meaningful stories about themselves, both to celebrate who they are and to connect with and help others.

As Ashley and I explored her own story, a struggle she's dealing with came up. There are times when she really wants to hide. To be invisible.

That's not ideal for a business owner.

She's got a gift that she's struggling to use, but her paradox isn't quite the Paradox of Talent (we'll focus on that in Curiosity #12 - Truth Bomb: We Undervalue our Talents). Instead, Ashley talked about the fear of being criticized and made fun of. She mentioned it as a holdover from some of her past interactions and relationships.

We Shouldn't Care what Others Think - Right?

As you'd probably expect from someone who lives in our independence worshipping culture, Ashley says she knows that she shouldn't care about other people's opinions. That if people don't like what she does, she doesn't need to work with them, and that's ok. She should be able to rise above their criticism, and feel successful because she knows what she's doing is awesome. Who needs them anyway!

When I asked Ashley about how she feels about her work and hiding right now, I was really interested to hear that she's finding it easier to come out of the shadows. She talked about her own journey, and doing some of the hard work of self discovery and personal growth.

You Need to Experience Worthiness to Feel it

Part of her recent journey to feeling successful has been cutting off or limiting relationships that weren't respectful, and creating and nurturing relationships with people who support her. Ashley said her confidence and feelings of being successful increased a lot when she found people who would treat her well. Her confidence in her business increased even more when she found other entrepreneurs who valued her, her attitude, and what she does.

She said it was like flipping a switch.

Once Ashley found some people who wanted to support her and who valued her, other people's opinions really DIDN'T matter very much. Instead of trying to persuade herself that criticism didn't matter, it just - really didn't.

It's true that you need to know you're worthy before you can feel worthy - (remember, that was the focus of Curiosity #1 - Truth Bomb: You Can't Earn Self-Worth) - but to experience love and belonging, you also need healthy relationships. Even if you know you're worthy of love and connection, if you're isolated or otherwise don't have the relationships you need, it might leave you feeling down in a way that erodes your sense of worth. One of the most important things to pay attention to is that sense that someone genuinely cares about you - and that you care about them as well. A feeling that someone cares about you personally is an important part of trust.

> That's the paradox of independence - **to be our most independent and resistant to rejection, we need our "soul family"**, a small group of people that we DO allow ourselves to depend on.

The Importance of a Soul Family

The idea of a "soul family" was solidified for me by my friend Christine. During a hard time in my life, she said I needed to embrace the friends who really want to support me. They are my soul family. Having a soul family means I never have to wonder if I'm loved, or if I belong. I have people who are personally invested in my success and well-being - and I'm personally invested in theirs.

One of the most important things I've learned about emotional health is the foundation of emotional health provided by that core group of people who really care. Make this at least a few people - having just one means you're likely to depend too much on that person to fulfill all of your needs. We'll dig deeper into the myth in our society that one person should be able to fulfill all your needs in Curiosity #7 - The Soul Mate Myth.

Being part of a mutually supportive group is critical to a sense of physical safety, the opposite of which can turn into a constant, underlying anxiety. We'll dig further into that, and the reason why being lonely feels like we're in physical danger, in Curiosity # 10 - The Paradox of Loneliness.

Your 'Real' Family Might not be Your People

It can be a difficult thing to realize that your family, the people who are "supposed" to care about you and your well-being, might not be willing or able to treat you well. I've talked about how difficult I found it to realize that about my brother in Curiosity #1 - You Can't Earn Self-Worth. I've also helped other people realize that since some members of their biological family are simply NOT people that can be counted on, that boundaries need to be put into place about what you will and won't ask of them.

Examining your relationships and recognizing who you can and can't count on for support is a very important step. It helps you understand what you need from relationships and how to create and nurture healthy ones. It might take awhile to realize that the lack of a healthy relationship can be way more about THEM than about you. And it can be hard to accept that it might not be in your power to "fix" the relationship.

Of course, your relatives COULD be part of your soul family, but unfortunately, for many of us we have some family members that don't offer us emotionally healthy support.

It's Important to Both Give and Take

Your soul family are those people that you can count on and who can count on you. It's important to realize we need to have relationships in which we can - and do - BOTH give and receive help. In their book Loneliness: Human Nature and the Need for Social Connection, John Cacioppo and William Patrick talk about the importance of what they call "mutually beneficial relationships". These are the relationships where we are able to both give and take. These are the relationships that add to our sense of safety and well-being, and that we need to nurture for a true feeling of success.

I've talked to many MANY women who find it really easy to give in relationships - yet it's crushingly hard for them to ask for any sort of help. Sometimes women feel like asking for help is selfish. Sometimes they feel like it's weakness. Sometimes it's because they've wrapped themselves up in helping others as a defence against facing that they DO need help or support. Often women have a huge identity as a "Helper" - so it's hard for them to step out of a helping role and accept being on the other side of the equation.

My Guelph Moms Supporting Moms group on Facebook is a really interesting example of giving and taking. I noticed that names were becoming familiar - and quite often I only noticed them asking for help or helping others, but seldom both. I ran a poll asking if people found it easier to help others, ask for help, or if they found both equal - and I got lots of responses for all of those options. It takes trust to be able to ask for help, but it also takes trust to offer it. It takes a belief that you have something of value to offer and that it will be appreciated.

Your soul family provides you a very solid foundation to stand on when it comes to withstanding the opinions of people outside that core group. When you know that you are loved and valued by people you personally care about, other people's criticism might still hurt - but it feels a lot more like a mosquito bite than a stab to the heart.

Resilience in the face of criticism is essential for not feeling like you need to please everyone. And when you don't feel like you have to please everyone? You can come out of the shadows, like Ashley.

Five Growing Questions about Independence:

1. Do you have a "soul family" - people who care about your well-being and you care about theirs in return? If so, list them.

2. Are you a people pleaser? If so, how would your life change if you stopped needing to please everyone?

3. Do you feel a disconnect between knowing you're worthy and feeling it? Where do you think this comes from?

4. Do you feel that some of your biological family is part of your soul family? Why or why not? How do you feel about this?

5. Do you find it easier to ask for help when you need it, or to offer help to others? Why do you think this is?

Independence Summary Question:

What was one thing you learned in this chapter about independence that you want to include in your personal definition of success? Write or dictate a note for yourself, or put it in the appropriate section of the journal provided (find out how to download the journal for free at http://tamsen.ca/paradoxjournalfree).

My glorification of independence and individualism made me an easy target for the myth of meritocracy, and overshadowed what in my heart I knew to be true: the deep interconnectedness I longed for with family, friends, colleagues, and even strangers is core to human survival. Interdependence is our lifeblood.

- Debby Irving

Curiosity #7 - The Soul Mate Myth

There is no such thing as a soulmate...And who would want there to be? I don't want half of a shared soul. I want my own damn soul.

- Rachel Cohn

Now that we've dealt with how important having a soul family is to our emotional well-being, let's tackle the soul mate myth - that one person should be able to fulfill all your needs. Having our needs met is a prerequisite for feeling satisfied and successful - and we'll be digging into universal needs in the last section, Creating Meaning. For now, realize that having our needs met often involves other people, and who we expect to meet those needs is important.

When I was a teenager, I was hooked on romance novels. I would take my allowance and go to a used book store where I could buy them for 10 cents and bring home bags of books. I loved reading stories of people finding "the one". Getting to the "happily ever after."

Relationships Aren't Something You Find

Of course, there are a lot of reasons why romance novels weren't the best way to learn about relationships. They're very heteronormative for one, and very focused on monogamy as being the expectation. They also focus on this idea of "the one" - of only one person being the perfect soul mate for you.

The main challenge in love - and life in general! - in romance novels seems to be "finding" the right one, your soul mate, and then staying patient until they realize you are THEIR soul mate. Now I'm married it's totally clear that committing to a relationship is the beginning of the story, not the end. You don't find a relationship, you build it - and it takes a lot of mutual work.

> That's the soul mate myth - there is one magical person out there who can fulfill all your needs, and all you need to do is find them to have a fantastic relationship and feel whole. Yet the truth is, **one person can't fulfill all your needs.**

Don't Expect One Person to Meet all Your Needs

I'm writing this just after celebrating Women's Day 2022 with a special event, and my friend Shanan joined us to talk about the importance of healthy relationships. We discussed what people believe about what makes a relationship successful. We talked about this idea of the soul mate, that we somehow should be able to have all of our needs met by one person, for our entire lives once we find them. None of us had experienced one person being able to fulfill all of our needs! We all need multiple people in our lives to have all our needs met - and sometimes, people who are just what we need at one time are people we need to let go later.

Right now my relationship with my son is the most rewarding - "successful" - relationship in my life. There are a lot of things I get out of my relationship with Tommy. One of the things that makes this relationship successful for me is that it puts me in situations that push me to grow and to be the best person I can!

Even though my relationship with my son is awesome, I still need adult friends. I let my son see that I have feelings and talk to him about them, but it wouldn't be fair to ask him to be a huge source of emotional support for me. He's 10, and that's an adult ask to me. My relationship with him fulfills a lot of my needs, but I don't expect it to fulfill all of them! And I do hope to have a relationship with my son for the rest of my life, but not all relationships last that long. And that's ok.

Soul Friends - for Awhile

There was a time in my friend Shanan's life when she became really close with a couple of her girlfriends. They had kids around the same age, and they would take vacations together. She and her friends would parent as a team, taking a lot of the pressure off of raising kids, and they trusted each other not only with their lives - with their kids' lives! Now that's trust.

Shanan remembers it as a time in her life when she felt absolutely supported and very loved. She had been married and divorced, and was building an independent life without a partner, but in her heart these two friends felt like soul mates. Unfortunately, it wasn't to last.

Several huge challenges hit Shanan all at once - her dad got sick with cancer, she was struggling in her relationship with her kids' dad, and she was being bullied at work. She decided to leave the corporate world and go into business for herself. Her two friends chose not to be supportive of her decision to build a business and not look for a "real" job. Shanan can see that her friends pushing her to reconsider self-employment was probably intended to be helpful - but it came across to her as critical and judgemental. And when she asked that they just drop the conversation, they wouldn't let it go. cancer, she was struggling in her relationship with her kids' dad, and she was being bullied at work. She decided to leave the corporate world and go into business for herself. Her two friends chose not to be supportive of her decision to leave a "real" job. Shanan can see that her friends pushing her to reconsider leaving a regular job was probably intended to be helpful - but it came across to her as critical and judgemental. And when she asked that they just drop the conversation, they wouldn't let it go.

The friendships ended.

It's painful for Shanan that friendships that were such a core part of her support network are gone - and that doesn't diminish the good times that they had. The duration of relationships is often taken as a sign of success - especially in romantic relationships. But we all know of married people who we imagine would be MUCH happier if they were to split - and many of us can remember relationships that we would have been better off out of sooner.

Here are some questions to ask yourself about soul mates, whether you believe in them, and whether believing in them is helpful to you:

Five Growing Questions about Soul Mates:

1. Do you believe in soul mates? Why or why not?

2. What to you makes a relationship successful?

3. Do you know what you need from your relationships? What is it?

4. Do you have someone you think of as "your person"? What needs do they help you meet? What needs don't they meet?

5. Have you ever been in a relationship with someone who saw "success" in a relationship differently than you did? What was that like for you? What did you learn?

Soul Mates Summary Question:

What was one thing you learned in this chapter about soul mates that you want to include in your personal definition of success? Write or dictate a note for yourself, or put it in the appropriate section of the journal provided (find out how to download the journal for free at http://tamsen.ca/paradoxjournalfree).

Some friends are for life, others are there to teach us about life.

- Neev Spencer

Curiosity #8 - The Paradox of Support

The most basic and powerful way to connect to another person is to listen. Just listen. Perhaps the most important thing we ever give each other is our attention.

- Rachel Naomi Remen

Wandering around the office maze a few days before my oral Master's defence, I was worrying at anyone who would stand still. "I'm terrified; I don't feel ready; What happened the last time someone failed this thing?!?!" What I heard were many versions of, "Don't worry, you'll do fine!"

But…

If I Could Have Stopped Worrying I Would Have Already!

Even though being told not to worry was supposed to help, it didn't. I couldn't do it! I couldn't just stop worrying. Also… I had just told people that I was scared, and even people who had gone through the same thing and been worried about defending their own thesis a month ago still didn't seem to really hear me. Or maybe they just weren't willing to listen?

Instead of feeling comforted and supported, I felt dismissed.

People Need to Feel Heard BEFORE You Offer Solutions

Part of having successful relationships is knowing what you need from others when you need emotional support - and how to give healthy emotional support when those you care about need it from you.

I spend a lot of time on Facebook, especially in my Guelph Moms Supporting Moms Facebook group. There are a lot of people asking for emotional support. I see this comment as a reply to someone talking about their struggles quite often - "You got this!"It's meant well, as an offering of support and faith. A statement that someone believes in you. And you know what? It's awesome, it's amazing to be told that someone believes that you can overcome your challenges.

Here's the thing - letting someone know you have faith in them to handle their own problems needs to come AFTER you listen to them. Otherwise, they'll end up feeling like I did before my defence - that you mean well, but you just don't get it. And often they'll also interpret you as saying that there's something wrong with them for feeling how they feel (or being willing to admit it). That's a huge betrayal of trust, and it's shocking that it often comes from trying to help someone feel better.

> That's the paradox of support - we're taught that to help someone we need to fix things for them. Instead, the **people who are struggling need to share their feelings and feel heard BEFORE starting to problem solve with them.**

Sometimes Life Sucks

You know what? Sometimes life really does just suck. When bad things happen it's ok to feel sad, afraid, angry, lonely… All of the painful feelings have their place in our experience. I wonder what would happen if, instead of trying to jump in to fix things, or to "make" people feel better, we started saying "Wow, it sounds like you're having a hard time. Tell me more about it." What if we acknowledged what people were feeling, that they're hurting, instead of saying "Stay strong!", "You GOT this!",

"Don't worry, tomorrow will be better!", or other things that really just say - don't feel bad.

I am trained in helping people overcome grief through the Grief Recovery Institute, and I'm often asked questions that make offering emotional support seem like something you can plan down to the last detail. What is the right thing to say? What should or shouldn't you do? If someone says they want to be alone, should you believe them?

Shift Your Focus from You to Them

There is a very important perspective shift that can help when we consider supporting someone emotionally - the focus shouldn't be on us or what we need to do. It's about the person who needs our emotional support, and what THEY need to do.

In general, the best place to start in offering someone healthy emotional support is to get them talking about their emotions, and to realize that it's safe for them to be honest with us. Then we need to pay attention. That means doing our best to give them ALL of our attention, and not to plan what we're going to say when it's our turn.

To many of you, giving your complete attention to what someone else is saying might seem easy. For me, it's really difficult. I've gained a lot from going through graduate school, but one of the negative things is that I was taught to NOT give 100% of my attention to the person speaking. When people would give presentations or teach a class, as students we were praised for having intelligent questions to ask in return. That meant we needed to pay attention to what was being said, but we also had to be analyzing everything said for weak points to bring up, and then also spending our mental resources remembering what those points were until it was our time to talk! That's not a recipe for helping someone feel heard.

There are definitely a lot of tips and additional things that you can think about for helping someone emotionally and having emotionally healthy relationships. But that's the biggest one - don't think that it's about you fixing the situation for someone, or fixing the person or their emotions. That's not your job, and not your place. I'll dare to say - even for your kids.

One of the greatest gifts we can give to someone who is in emotional pain is to sit there with them. We don't have to be in the same type of pain, although to the extent we care about them we will be feeling with them. They may not be ready to talk, or to know what to say. Do your best to let that be ok.

Sometimes We Don't Know What to Do - and That's Ok

Really, sometimes you can just say "I don't know what to say, or what to do, but I'm here and I care and I want to help."

I walked into my shared office one day to see Natalie, the new graduate student in our lab, sitting at her desk, in tears.

Ummmm... Totally awkward.

I really didn't know what to do. I put my stuff down on my desk, and thought about just walking out again. Instead, I told her "I don't know you well enough to know what you want me to do, but I want to help. If you want to be alone, I'll leave. If you want to talk, I'll stay and listen." We ended up talking - Natalie was really upset about something that had happened in one of her classes. Eventually, to blow off steam, I handed her my gloves, and told her if she was angry she could throw them across the room.

We did that for awhile - eventually our hats and her gloves also made it into the mix of stuff being thrown at the wall. Natalie would throw them, and I would fetch them back, and she'd throw them again. We gradually moved from anger to laughter, and Natalie became one of my best friends in grad school. That was long before I trained in emotional education, but I inadvertently did a few things that helped.

I acknowledged Natalie's feelings, and I let her talk about them. I didn't try to tell her not to feel a certain way.

I also let Natalie know that I wanted to help but didn't know what to do, what she would prefer - and I let her tell me. Sometimes when we don't know what to do we should just 'fess up, and go from there. Yes, it's true that sometimes when people are upset and grieving, asking them what they want is an additional burden. If we have a reasonable guess, then offering help in a concrete way like "would it help if I took your dog for a walk?" can be really helpful. Yet if we don't have a clue, it's better to ask than to do nothing.

As I listened to Natalie talk about what she was going through, and I stayed in the moment, I got clues about how I could help her. I have no idea what possessed me to suggest she start throwing things, it's not something I typically do. It just... Seemed right at the time. I think that's the most valuable thing I've learned from my emotional work - it's just that staying present, listening and paying attention, is the best way we have to help someone struggling with painful feelings.

Paying Attention can be HARD

I know that for a lot of people, listening to someone else with your full attention sounds really easy. Many people are better at listening than I am. In case it's difficult for you, I want you to know you're not alone.

Giving my full attention to someone who is talking has been a really tough skill for me to develop. Thing is, I've been trained for a long time to do the opposite in graduate school. Students are expected to have something smart to say in reply to what someone else is saying. When I do that, a huge chunk of my attention is in my own head, not on the person I'm trying to connect with. After practicing devoting my full attention to someone when they're talking, I've managed to not have something to say occasionally when it's my turn to talk. I consider that a huge victory for me!

After You Listen and Connect, THEN it's Ok to Move On

Just like Natalie and I moved on from talking about her feelings to throwing things and then laughing about it, there can be a time when it's ok to move on and to try to change our feelings or solve the problem.

As I've heard it said - "Sometimes we have to wade through the emotional swamp - but we shouldn't set up camp there." Yet, make sure the person you're trying to support really feels heard first, or moving on to changing feelings or finding solutions will feel like a dismissal of how they feel, not help.

Five Growing Questions about Support:

1. Was there anything in this chapter that surprised you about healthy emotional support?

2. When is the last time you needed emotional support from someone? What happened? Did you end up feeling supported, dismissed, or something else?

3. How difficult is it for you to stay present and listen when someone is talking to you about their feelings? Why?

4. How strong is your urge to fix other people's problems? How difficult would it be to listen to their feelings first?

5. What version of "that sucks" could you use that suits you, but also isn't dismissive of someone's feelings if they share something painful with you?

Support Summary Question:

What was one thing you learned in this chapter about support that you want to include in your personal definition of success? Write or dictate a note for yourself, or put it in the appropriate section of the journal provided (find out how to download the journal for free at http://tamsen.ca/paradoxjournalfree).

I have learned now that while those who speak about one's miseries usually hurt, those who keep silence hurt more.

- C. S. Lewis

Curiosity #9 - Truth Bomb: You Need to Be the Friend You Want

The only way to have a friend is to be one.

- Ralph Waldo Emerson

I mentioned in the self-compassion chapter (Curiosity #2 - The Paradox of Self-Compassion) that one tool for practicing self-compassion is to consider yourself as a friend. So, this chapter is important for creating healthy relationships with other people, but it's also important for creating self-worth too!

Friends are something most of us have from our earliest years - but what is friendship, exactly? And what makes for healthy friendships rather than toxic ones? We're going to talk about the importance of being able to trust that someone is on your side, and the importance of creating and maintaining healthy boundaries, both with others and with yourself.

Trust that Someone is On Your Side

There are at least three important types of trust. Trust in ability and integrity are both important, and we focussed on trust in ability in Curiosity #4 - The Confidence Myth. The third type of trust is the the one that I think has the biggest impact on our friendships. That's trust in someone's benevolence toward you - that belief that someone has your best interests in mind. We trust people when they believe they're on our side! If we believe someone takes our well-being personally, if we feel cared about as an individual, it's a lot easier to feel safe with them than if we don't trust they are on our side.

Did you have a favourite teacher while you were in school? I'm guessing if you did, that you felt they cared about you as a person, and you weren't just another student to them. Contrast this with the way a judge in a courtroom is supposed to be - they are supposed to be impartial, to not take sides. If you're in their courtroom, you're not supposed to matter as a person. Not exactly an image that gives me the warm fuzzies, how about you?

The pandemic has brought many changes, and many of them not so fun - but one of the good changes is that I've become a lot closer to two of my friends, Audrey and Theresa. We have regular Zoom chats - and this relationship wouldn't have been possible if we were focusing on in person relationships, since we all live in different countries! It's been invaluable for us to have good friends that we can count on during these challenging times, and knowing that we care deeply about each other is a key part of why we feel close. We trust one another.

One thing that my friendship with Audrey and Theresa has brought home to me is the importance of boundaries. Boundaries are important in a friendship to keep it healthy. Healthy friendships also allow us to work on our boundaries with ourselves and other people!

Set and Maintain Healthy Boundaries

Having healthy boundaries is important, but it's also a little catch-phrasy these days. So let's make it clear exactly what we're talking about. Boundaries are simply what you say yes to and what you say no to. Boundaries are standards you set - but you also have to maintain them. What do you allow, and what don't you?

There is an important link between boundaries and trust. How you treat other people is one of the best ways we have to guess what your values are - whether we see you as having integrity. Someone's behaviour is also evidence we use to understand if someone has our best interests at heart, or whether they will turn on us if they have the chance. And it's not only about how people treat us, but how we see them treating other people and themselves.

Brené Brown talks about this kind of indirect trust breaking in her book Braving the Wilderness. What happens f you come to me and want to gossip about someone, telling me things I'm not supposed to know, or badmouthing them behind their back? I'm going to assume you're talking about me behind my back too, or dishing any secrets that I ask you to keep to yourself. You might be doing it in an attempt to create a bond with me, but what really happens is that betraying someone else's trust destroys my trust in you.

There's a big difference between this type of gossip and coming to a friend to talk about a difficult relationship. One is about sharing what YOU'RE struggling with, the other is delighting in someone else's misfortune. Not the same thing at all.

Some people haven't been taught how to have healthy boundaries. Being raised to allow unhealthy behaviours and accept them as normal is a HUGE problem that many of us have to overcome. It is possible to set boundaries without needing to be rude or confrontational about it. It's definitely possible that politely setting boundaries can provoke an impolite reaction, but you don't have to respond in kind.

> The Truth Bomb: You need to be the friend you want. To have healthy relationships you need to **figure out what true friendship is to you, and then to BE that,** to yourself and carefully selected others who return the friendship.

Can You Trust Yourself?

You need to trust that someone else has your well-being in mind to fully trust them. You also need to treat yourself just as well, or you'll end up not trusting yourself. Not trusting yourself can chip away at your sense of self-worth and safety.

Boundaries are important to set for yourself. Decide how you're willing to treat other people, and yourself. If you've heard people talk about "taking the high road", that's it - not allowing yourself to justify engaging in unhealthy, hurtful behaviour simply because someone else does first.

Setting standards for your own behaviour is also important if you identify as a "people pleaser". If you're willing to bend yourself into a pretzel shape to avoid confrontation, you're probably sacrificing your own values in the moment. This can erode your trust in yourself, especially if it happens frequently. Use the questions at the end of this chapter to identify your challenges with having healthy relationships, and what you would like to work on most.

True Friendship Takes Courage

Many of us need emotional support from our relationships. How to give and receive healthy emotional support deserves it's own chapter, and you can find it in Curiosity #8 - The Paradox of Support. For now, I want to acknowledge that healthy friendships require us being willing to be honest and to show our true selves. Being seen means being vulnerable, so it takes courage. No matter how well we are treated in our relationships, if we are too scared to show who we really are, we'll never feel truly loved. If you're finding this a challenge, you may need to spend more time working on your self-worth (rereading Curiosity #1 - Truth Bomb: You Can't Earn Self-Worth might help).

Five Growing Questions about Friendship:

1. What is a very important boundary for you to set in your relationships so you feel safe?

2. What is one way you were raised to have healthy boundaries?

3. What is one way you were raised to have unhealthy boundaries?

4. What relationships are important for your personal definition of success?

5. Is there a relationship that has boundaries you need to work on so that it feels healthier? What could that look like for you?

Friendship Summary Question:

What was one thing you learned in this chapter about friendship that you want to include in your personal definition of success? Write or dictate a note for yourself, or put it in the appropriate section of the journal provided (find out how to download the journal for free at http://tamsen.ca/paradoxjournalfree).

'No.' is a complete sentence.

- Anne Lamont

Curiosity #10 - The Paradox of Loneliness

I am lonely, yet not everybody will do. I don't know why, some people fill the gaps and others emphasize my loneliness.

- Anaïs Nin

My good friend Theresa lives in Michigan, close to Detroit. If you know the weather patterns there, it's no surprise to you that getting out in the winter can take some effort. It takes Theresa more effort than for many of us, because she uses a wheelchair and snow can be a challenge!

Theresa and I were talking about how winter a few years ago just seemed really hard - lots of sickness, losses in our families, it was hard to get motivated to do work. Then Theresa started talking about just how difficult it was to get out and be around people, even though she knew she needed to be around people to feel better. She needed to leave the house to feel successful and that she was living the life she wanted to live!

Theresa is normally very sociable, but people just... Seemed like too much effort. The people she ended up being around weren't really "her people" - they weren't supportive or helpful. Somehow, being around people made things worse, not better. Theresa didn't feel connected, even when she made the effort to get out with the goal of connecting!

It Feels Safer to Stay Lonely

It seemed much safer to Theresa, and far easier, just to stay at home, alone. To stay lonely.

That's the paradox of loneliness - the more we need social connection, the scarier it is and harder it is to be around people and allow ourselves to connect.

Research shows that loneliness can be worse for our health than smoking or being obese. If you want to read more about this and find out some of the research around loneliness, I highly recommend "Loneliness: Human Nature and the Need for Social Connection" by John T. Cacioppo and William Patrick. The need to be around others is hardwired into us - it's a survival mechanism based on how humans evolved. We're prepared to live like hunter gatherers did for most of our human history.

We Used to Need Each Other… So We Still Do

Hunter gatherers live in groups, and members count on each other for survival. One idea is that emotions evolved in order to help us connect and stay in groups. Loneliness possibly developed as a survival mechanism - if you didn't feel connected to your group members, you'd better take care of that, fast. If you didn't want to die, that is.

So the feeling of loneliness might be explained by that - it's a survival mechanism from our past. But why on earth when we feel lonely, would we be put off by the idea of being around other people and being less lonely?

I've Got Your Back and You've Got Mine

If you've ever seen it, watching giraffes try to drink is pretty funny. They kind of have to splay their legs really awkwardly to get their head down low enough to get some water. It not only looks gawky, but it also looks like a pretty vulnerable position. If there was a lion or other predator nearby, it's not a good position to be in. But giraffes need water sometimes, or they'll die.

Giraffes often travel in groups - and if you watch them, you'll notice that they sort of team up - all the giraffes don't drink at once. There's usually one or two with their heads held high, scanning the environment for threats. That's an awesome benefit of being in a group, if everyone watches out for one another. The giraffes working together to watch out for predators don't have to see everything themselves, if there is more than one watching out at the same time. Some get to take a break and get a drink, and can rely on others to help keep them safe.

A giraffe alone has the choice of watching, or drinking, and can't do both at the same time. People who feel lonely start to feel stressed out, just like that poor lonely giraffe probably does. We don't feel like anyone has our backs. We have to do all the looking out for ourselves. Part of our reaction to being alone is to get extra vigilant - we become extra sensitive to the possibility of something being a threat. We need to do that to stay safe, at least our old wiring from the hunter gatherer days spurs us to feel like we need to be on guard. And we don't have "new" wiring, we're stuck with the old stuff. Since we're the only ones who will notice something that could hurt us, we have to spend a lot of our time watching out.

This process of increasing our vigilance when we're lonely results in loneliness being translated into a sense of being physically unsafe. In our current world, that doesn't make sense. But with our evolutionary history, it makes perfect sense. If we are alone, we are much more likely to die.

People Can be Dangerous

A second thing that results from being extra aware that something could be a threat, is that sometimes threats come from other people! It's a double-edged sword - we need to be around people to feel less lonely, but we also need to make sure that the people we choose to be around won't hurt us. Since we're busy looking for things that are dangerous, it's easy to take interactions (which are often ambiguous) and see them as threatening.

So, Theresa was experiencing all of this. She was lonely, so she felt physically unsafe, which meant she felt leaving her house was somewhat dangerous. Added to that, when she was around people, she just couldn't relax and trust them, because she was busy looking for threats. Guess what - when you're busy looking for threats, you tend to find them. We need to connect, but we go out and see all sorts of negative reactions from people. So we go back and hide at home. As Theresa found, it can take a long time to come out of a funk like this.

If you are lonely, here are some things you can try:

Tip #1 - Avoid Hostility and Conflict

First, if you do have people in your life that you absolutely trust, try being around them first. Avoid things like family gatherings where hostility is known to erupt! You need evidence that people can be safe, not more evidence that they aren't.

This is a case where you can really benefit from explicitly identifying and nurturing your "soul family". I go into this in Curiosity #6 - The Paradox of Independence, so I won't repeat it here. Being able to share that you're struggling with people you trust can really help.

Tip #2 - Be Aware You're Looking for Danger

Second, be aware that human interactions are full of events that can be interpreted in lots of different ways. If you're lonely, you're more likely to interpret these mixed messages as threatening. Someone is curt with you? Your response when you're not lonely might be "Wow, SOMEONE'S having a bad day! Glad it's not me." When you're feeling lonely and isolated? Your response might be more like "Wow, what on earth did I do to piss THEM off? Why do they hate me so much? What are they going to do to get back at me?"

Tip #3 - Take Action Quickly

When you're in this downward loneliness and anxiety spiral, it can be hard to come up for air. Do your best to notice when you start to feel lonely, and do something about it as soon as possible. Have that phone chat, go for coffee, connect with your soul family. Do something to help yourself realize that there are other people who really care and who want to have your back.

Five Growing Questions about Loneliness:

1. Are you surprised how large and negative an effect loneliness can have on your physical health? What does this bring up for you?

2. Describe a time in your life you were lonely. How did you get out of it, or are you still in it?

3. Have you noticed that when you're lonely, it's hard to be around people? What does this feel like for you?

4. Does knowing that being lonely can make someone afraid of being around people change how you want to reach out to people who might be lonely? What might you do differently?

5. Frosh Week at university can be seen as an attempt to integrate new students into the community before they get lonely. What are other ways that organizations, cultures, neighbourhoods, etc. try to head off loneliness? Do you think they are effective? Why or why not?

Loneliness Summary Question:

What was one thing you learned in this chapter about loneliness that you want to include in your personal definition of success? Write or dictate a note for yourself, or put it in the appropriate section of the journal provided (find out how to download the journal for free at http://tamsen.ca/paradoxjournalfree).

> Crocodiles are easy. They try to kill and eat you. People are harder. Sometimes they pretend to be your friend first.
>
> - Steve Irwin

Creating Healthy Relationships: Summary

You must find the courage to leave the table if respect is no longer being served.

- Tene Edwards

The Creating Healthy Relationships section is about creating and maintaining healthy connections with other people, while not sacrificing your relationship with yourself. In this summary section, we're checking back in to see what's changed with the new insights you have gained.

You may be able to answer these questions right away. You may also want to reexamine your answers to the review questions from each chapter in this section, and decide on which feels the most important to include in your personal definition of success right now.

Remember that there is no "right" or "wrong" answer. If you're having trouble deciding, don't stress about it. There will be time to decide what to focus on when you're deciding on your action plan - and I'll introduce some strategies to help you deal with overwhelm if you're still having trouble deciding then!

Review Questions:

Check in - has reading this section and answering the questions changed any of your answers?

1. Definition review question: What does "healthy relationship" mean to you right now, after reading this section?

2. Self-assessment review question: How healthy do you think your relationships are right now, after reading this section?

3. Goal review question: What is the main thing you want to change about the health of your relationships after reading this section?

4. Achievement review question: How will you know you've achieved your relationship health goal?

Love of others and love of ourselves are not alternatives. On the contrary, an attitude of love toward themselves will be found in all those who are capable of loving others.

- Erich Fromm

Section: Creating Meaning

We have overstretched our personal boundaries and forgotten that true happiness comes from living an authentic life fuelled with a sense of purpose and balance.

- Kathleen Hall

There's a reason I'm calling this section "Creating Meaning" rather than finding it. Just "finding" meaning doesn't happen for most people. I'll be sharing my own stories of how I connected with my passions and purpose, and the stories of other people too! There will be strategies that you can try, both in this section and in the Redefining Success section.

The first roadblock on your way to creating meaning and a successful life that we'll discuss in this section is trying to find your "one true passion". Some other hurdles we'll discuss include trying to create the elusive "work-life balance", and needing to make decisions when you have so many options that deciding between them seems impossible. We'll dig into why most of us don't value our own talents, and we'll discuss how fear can creep into our journey and stop us from doing what we need to do to feel successful.

Creating Meaning Orienting Questions:

1. Definition question: What does it mean to have a "meaningful life" to you right now?

2. Self-assessment question: What is the current level of meaning in your life right now?

3. Goal question: What is the main thing you want to change about the level of meaning you have in your life right now?

4. Achievement question: How will you know you've achieved your level of meaning goal?

The problem, often not discovered until late in life, is that when you look for things in life like love, meaning, motivation, it implies they are sitting behind a tree or under a rock. The most successful people in life recognize, that in life they create their own love, they manufacture their own meaning, they generate their own motivation.

- Neil deGrasse Tyson

Curiosity #11 - The One Passion Myth

A specialized life is portrayed as the only path to success, and it's highly romanticized in our culture.

- Emilie Wapnick

My friend Susan Gentilcore believes that it's possible for everyone to discover their purpose and live it every day. I invited Susan, the creator of All Things Preserved, to speak at an event I organized for Women's Day. If there's one thing that comes across very quickly about Susan, it's that she's passionately dedicated to environmentalism and, as she puts it, being kind to the planet that we all live on. In deep curiosity about how she came to have such a clear sense of purpose, and in respect of the fact she had arranged her life so that she could actively live that purpose every day, I asked her to share her story about how she came to connect with that deep sense of meaning.

I mentioned to Susan that telling her story was enough - I didn't necessarily expect her to be able to help everyone find the same thing for themselves. I knew she would be an inspiration and start a really interesting conversation. When she said she also had a lot of suggestions about how other people COULD find their own sense of purpose, I was thrilled! One of the most amazing insights Susan shared was the fact that she doesn't think that it's true you will have one single, enduring passion and that you will only feel successful and like you're living a purposeful life if you arrange your life around it. There are lots of ways to live a successful, meaningful life!

> That's the One Passion Myth - that to feel successful and fulfilled, all you need to do is find your one true, enduring passion, and follow it. **For most of us, we don't have just one passion, and need more than to find passion to feel successful, we need to create our purpose.**

There's Sometimes Not JUST ONE PASSION in Our Lives

Growing up, Susan was taught that you have one passion in your life, and until you find "it" you will never feel fulfilled. She's found that just wasn't true for her. Susan has had multiple passions since she was a child - she's a maker, a nature lover, and an educator. She did all of these things at different ways at different times, but none of these things alone resulted in her feeling fulfilled. If Susan was making things but not in an environmentally sustainable way, she didn't feel good about it.

Sometimes to feel fulfilled you need to engage multiple passions at one time, like Susan - but it also might be true that your passions change over time.

Passions Can Change

If you have an employment history, you might find it useful to examine the parts of previous jobs that you liked and what you didn't, and try to figure out why.

Sometimes income needs to be your focus. The stage of life you're in and your circumstances matter. Sometimes you can bring your passions into your work, but not always. Susan helped reduce paper waste at one of her jobs, which helped fulfill her passion as an environmentalist while in a job that had nothing to do with helping the environment. It helped her feel that in her own little way she could make her work environment a better place for the environment - and that's huge for her. She's proud of it.

When Susan was talking about passions changing, I could relate. When my son was a newborn, it really felt like my only passion and my sole purpose was keeping him alive - that took all my time and energy! It took awhile before I could re-incorporate other things that are important to me into my life.

There are also people whose passions are serial - they are very passionate about something until they feel they have mastered it - and then it's boring. They're done and ready to tackle a new challenge. Jennifer Grigg describes this experience in Momtellectual episodes 102 & 103 (You can find them at tamsen.ca/momtellectual102 and tamsen.ca/momtellectual103). She had her dream job training firefighters, yet as soon as she felt she had that job nailed down, she felt she needed to move on. Jennifer recognized this as a recurring pattern in her life, and was very relieved that this was something that other people experienced too!

Passions Can Seem Small

Growing up, Susan didn't really feel that her love of making was respected. She was just someone who "likes to make things". Still, making always brought her joy (which is one of the best ways to know that something is a passion for you!) Now making is the main part of her business, and she told us that even when she has to stay up late to finish an order it still brings her joy.

Susan says it's not necessarily a negative that passions can seem small. Your passions might seem small, either a small part of your life, or not all that important to other people, but still be really important to YOU. And Susan is definitely now recognized and respected as an entrepreneur and a maker with an environmental focus. Her son often will go to her and ask if they can make something rather than buy it, and she's a similar resource for Shanan and other friends! When people ask her to help them make something rather than buy it, Susan says that she's done her work in passing on her passions and understanding about why they're important.

A DIY Passionate Life

Susan never sat down to purposefully create a meaningful life by combining her passions of making, nature, and nontraditional teaching. This career path certainly wasn't listed as a career anywhere! Susan was always told as a kid that being a maker could never bring in money or be a job. She ended up creating her career herself, and she sort of fell into it, making things that people wanted and were willing to pay for. She recalls saying to herself "I think this is a business - is this a thing? It's not, you can't look it up - but it's a thing I do now." Being self employed isn't an easy road, and Susan doesn't automatically recommend it to everyone - but it has given her an opportunity to embrace all of the things that she loves.

She not only has recognized her passions, but Susan used them to create her purpose - Living a zero waste lifestyle and being kind to the planet. In her work she sells earth friendly products, especially to replace single use plastics, and teaches people how to be kinder to the planet and how to make some of these products themselves. Susan not only has her purpose and has it as a big picture guide, but also lives it every day.

It may seem like an impossible goal for you to live your purpose in as intense and full a way as Susan does - but keep in mind she built it slowly, one piece at a time. She provides some hints about how to start which I'll share with you after we discuss how to identify your passions in the first place.

Questions to Help You Find Your Passions

Susan emphasizes that finding "your passion" can be really hard - finding "your passions" plural can be a lot easier. There are a ton of quizzes and tests out there to help you identify your passions - but Susan suggests that it can be easier to find your passions by looking at small parts of yourself. And remember - you're not looking for something that is huge, or appears in every part of your life - it can be something that seems small.

What brings YOU joy?

Some questions Susan suggested to help you find your passions:

- Remember a time you were exhausted but happy.
- Remember something you loved to do as a kid.
- What do your friends say lights you up?
- What would you do if you didn't have to show up for work today?
- What is the last story you told someone about yourself?

If you have ever felt connected with passion and joy in your life, those questions might help you reconnect!

What if You Need NEW Passions?

I love how Susan's passions have endured and grown since she was little. Many of the questions she suggests for finding your passions reflect that - they are ways of looking at the past for clues about what might bring you joy now. That can be hugely helpful for sure - yet for some of us, the past isn't the best place to look.

For me, my passions as a kid were reading, knitting, crocheting, and watching tv. I still read frequently, but I don't knit, crochet, or watch tv these days, and I have a lot of passions now that were definitely NOT things I got joy out of as a kid. I love writing now, but I didn't then - I could read all day, but I never felt the pull to write. I love psychology, and incorporate it into almost everything I do. It wasn't something I ever considered doing as a career, it never even occurred to me until after I was in university and took Psych 101 as an elective.

Ironically, as a teenager I remember discussing "what I would do when I grew up" with my mom, and she said I should be a teacher. I told her she was crazy - I was painfully shy, and my worst nightmare was having to talk in front of a bunch of people. When I started graduate school I was forced to teach - and now I love it, but I HATED it and was terrified to get up in front of a class for years. I never would have done it had I felt I had a choice.

Stumbling Into Passion

One of my biggest passions these days is being a community builder. I get joy every day out of running my Guelph Moms Supporting Moms Facebook group. We're currently in our 7th year, and I get a huge sense of satisfaction knowing that through that group, local moms get to help one another and feel connected to a community at a time when it's easy to feel isolated and lonely. It's been even more needed in the pandemic. Starting that group was just something I tried because it seemed to be needed, and no one else was putting their hand up to to it. I had gone through a rough time when I was a new mom myself, and so I did know that I wanted to help other moms, but I didn't really know what was involved in running a group - and I had no idea if I would be good at it, or enjoy it.

If you find yourself not being able to identify your current passions, the best suggestion I have for you is to be open to trying some new things. You just might find a key to your joy. And again, like Susan said, you don't need to look for something HUGE that you can incorporate into your life, and build your whole life around. There are a lot of ways you can do this, here are some suggestions:

- Pay attention to your joy in your daily life. Feel a moment of joy? Enjoy it as it happens, and also try to figure out how to recreate it. Was your joy sparked by what you were doing? Who you were with? Because you were learning? Because you created something? Because you were using your talents? Look for patterns in your joy.

- If you have a bucket list of things you want to try, go to it and schedule some things and DO them as soon as you can.

- Has someone you love invited you to try something and you've resisted? Give it a try. My son was excited to have me play Minecraft™ with him - and I didn't want to. I finally decided to try - I LOVE it now. It's a fun thing my son and I get to do together often, and it's also a valuable tool to start conversations with him. And honestly, I play on my own quite often - Minecraft™ is awesome.

- If you're asked to do something new in your job, consider saying yes, especially if you usually say no. Of course, consider your time and energy resources, but this can be a great way of trying new things and also potentially increasing your value to the company. Make sure it's not just busywork, but something that could be useful for you and your career.

- Ask your friends what they do for a hobby or when they have a few free minutes. Do they play a video game? Do puzzles or crafts? Cook? Garden? Would they be willing to share with you, show you the ropes? Even if you don't end up enjoying the activity, you got the side benefit of spending some time with a friend.

- Look in your area for workshops, classes, meetings. It's also a chance to meet new people. If you'd rather bond with a friend than meet new people, arrange to sign up with a buddy. You can do this online too!

- Minecraft™. Have I mentioned Minecraft™? Try Minecraft™, or some other type of game. Sometimes your passions really can be about having fun and not changing the world.

You Know Your Passions - Now What?!

I agree with Susan when she says adding passion to your life can start in a small way. Instead of trying to immediately demolish your current life and rebuild your life around your identified passions - consider how you can channel one of your passions into one small area of your life at a time. This idea of starting small isn't meant to diminish the importance of your passions - but most of us aren't in a position to totally upend our lives. Some of us still need jobs that will pay our bills, and can't currently see how our passions will bulk up our wallets.

Many people also keep their work and their passions fairly separate. It's totally ok to have a job that pays your bills and to satisfy your passions elsewhere. That works best for a lot of people. Susan suggested some areas of your life you could consider bringing your passions into: your family or another specific group of people, a situation, your job. See the impact that it makes on the people involved, the situation, and especially on you - your joy and sense of fulfillment. If the effects are helpful - continue it. And it doesn't need to grow if YOU don't need it to.

Susan asked us to remember - our passions might carry forward without our even knowing. Making other people aware of the good you're doing and aware of what your passions are, it will spur them on to ask the questions of themselves, embrace yours, look for others, and applaud people who are making a difference through their passions.

From Passion to Purpose

If your passions are what bring you joy, your purpose is what brings you fulfillment and satisfaction. Your passions are personal and what you want to have in your own life - your purpose is about the change you want to see in the world, what you want to bring to others.

Put simply - passion is about your emotion - purpose is the why.

What is the change you want to make in the world?

Try filling in the sentence, "It should be easier to ___________ than to __________."

Susan might say "It should be easier to be kind to the planet than to harm it." She has used her passions for nature, the environment, and teaching to help other people make sometimes difficult transitions to reducing single use plastics and paper to using products - and reusing products - that are kind to the planet. I say "It should be easier to feel whole and to live with a sense of purpose than to feel lost and broken." I do a lot of different things, but they are all under the umbrella of increasing confidence, which is a sense of trust and safety. It can take awhile to get clear on a statement like this, but what change would you like to see in the world? And what could this look like?

Susan described how she knows if she has fulfilled her purpose - if people consider what things can be repurposed for before sending them to the landfill, or if they figure out how something wanted can be made from repurposed materials rather than purchased, she's done something good.

Five Growing Questions about Passions and Purpose:

1. What are your passions? Which ones do you think you need to include in your personal definition of success?

2. What is your purpose statement? Fill in the sentence, "It should be easier to ___________ than to __________."

3. How important is it to you that the way you make money and your passions/purpose are the same? How similar are they now?

4. How have your passions changed over time? What do you think prompted these changes? What is something that could happen that would shift your passions again?

5. Is there someone in your life who you feel is really in touch with their passions and purpose? Can you state their passions and purpose clearly? What effect has this had on their life?

Passions and Purpose Summary Question:

What was one thing you learned in this chapter about passions and purpose that you want to include in your personal definition of success? Write or dictate a note for yourself, or put it in the appropriate section of the journal provided (find out how to download the journal for free at http://tamsen.ca/paradoxjournalfree).

> Don't ask yourself what the world needs; ask yourself what makes you come alive. And then go and do that. Because what the world needs is people who have come alive.
>
> - Howard Thurman

> **This chapter is dedicated to the memory of Susan Gentilcore, an inspirational woman who lived her passions and purpose every day.**

T

Curiosity #12 - Truth Bomb: We Undervalue Our Talents

From the cradle to the cubicle, we devote more time to our shortcomings than to our strengths.

- Tom Rath

Often when we're trying to build successful lives, we expect it to be difficult - so we miss what's right in front of our faces.

I have a wonderful, amazing friend named Audrey. I'm sad that she's moved far away from me here in Canada and lives in Scotland now, but we've started catching up regularly through video chats. As I'm writing this it's almost Christmas, and just now she was telling me about her plans for the holiday. Audrey has met some wonderful people lately, and they are quickly becoming good friends. For various reasons, they don't go to family on Christmas day. She found out that they would probably be together, and as one friend put it, would probably "eat dodgy takeaway" as none of them are particularly capable cooks. If there's one thing Audrey is great at, it's cooking.

Actually, Audrey is great at a TON of things. In addition to planning a delicious meal, she's very crafty, and she's making handmade presents for everyone. She's thoughtful and kind, and she's using her considerable intellect and problem solving skills to figure out how she can help everyone she's invited for Christmas day feel loved, cherished, and taken care of. We talked about how she's making handmade lotions, and not only that - how she's making them even more special by customizing the scents to her friends' preferences and personalities. We talked about how she's not doing a traditional turkey, but she thought it would be more in people's taste to do steak instead. She decided to make a cheesecake for dessert - then remembered that one of the guests is lactose intolerant, so she baked a caramel apple pie at the last minute so he wouldn't be dessertless!

And continually as we talked, Audrey downplayed her talent.

The cooking? "Oh, it will be easy, and it's not a big deal". The lotions? "It's kind of fun deciding how someone will smell, and it's nice to personalize things". The baking an extra dessert so that a friend felt considered and special? "Oh, I just whipped up a pie at the last minute." Of course, what Audrey was saying totally rang the "Paradox of Talent" bell for me!

I mentioned to Audrey that probably the Christmas meal she was going to prepare, although easy for her, would mean a lot to the friends eating it. "But it's not a big deal! Just a really simple dinner." I told her my perspective - that although maybe it was a 1 or 2 out of a 10 scale of effort for her, because she's an amazing cook, and enjoys cooking and baking - the difference between her meal and a "dodgy takeaway" was HUGE! I wanted her to appreciate that her talents, her gifts, and the things she was choosing to give to other people weren't just about what it cost her. I wanted her to see that even thought she didn't see it as costing her much, and even though she enjoyed doing those things, it didn't mean that they weren't worth a LOT to the people receiving the benefits of her talents.

We Underestimate the Value of Our Talents

So that's the challenge, then - those things that we find it the easiest to do, that we get joy from doing, we often think are TOO easy and fun. We sometimes can't even see the things we're good at, and usually can't fully appreciate the value they provide when we use our talents to help others. What tends to happen is that we look to things we find DIFFICULT to demonstrate that we can offer value. We might struggle, but since this work is hard, it's what we think we need to do to be successful, to be doing something "real".

And since we're struggling, we don't have a good time doing our work. We also don't do our best work, because we're not fully using our talents.

> That's the Truth Bomb: We underestimate our talents. When we're truly talented, it makes something easy, and so **the talented don't value what they are gifted at**. As a result, most of us shy away from using our unique blend of talents to bring amazing things into the world.

I was at a retreat for personal growth a few years ago, and a really interesting instructor named Chantal had us visualize ourselves as a pear tree. She really solidified the paradox of talent for me. I don't know if I can do justice to her description, but try this thought experiment:

There's that bountiful pear tree, right near a busy path. If you wait here awhile, you'll notice that travellers often stop at the pear tree. Sometimes they just enjoy the shade for a moment, or the wonderful smell of the pears. Most of the time though, the pause turns into picking and eating. Watch their faces - their expressions of joy might be so intense they make you laugh as you share their pure happiness at the experience of tasting the juicy, sweet, intensely flavourful pears.

Now follow me here - You are also a pear tree.

Like the tree near the path, you find it easy to make pears. For you, pears are simple, and the pears you make are delicious. And yes, some people are apple trees, or peach trees - there are lots of different things that we can be good at. The problem is, that that's where the similarity tends to stop.

The pear tree doesn't question whether making pears is worthwhile.

We Interpret Easy as Having No Value

A pear tree doesn't feel inadequate that it doesn't make apples - or that it can't make a whole fruit salad, for that matter. But people? What we can do easily - It's easy. That means it's too easy, and can never be good enough. What tends to happen is that we're pear trees, and if we're lucky we might choose to make a few pears in our spare time, but we spend the rest of the time trying to make apples. Like Audrey, we downplay the value of what we find easy, where our talents are. We look for work that is hard so that we know it has value.

One problem with focusing on doing things that we find difficult, is that there will be someone out there who finds what we struggle with easy. How we're trying to create value with difficult work - that's their talent. They find it easy, and it looks effortless, and they are "naturally" better at it than we might ever be, even with immense effort. That results in us feeling inadequate as we work and struggle to achieve mediocrity.

Some Talents ARE Valued More by Others

It's also not quite so simple as what we find easy we don't see as valuable - there is also a cultural layer to this. I think there are at least 2 related challenges in finding our talents valuable - needing to have things that are concrete and therefore measurable, and also that we tend to devalue "soft skills", or the things that work at a social level to keep relationships helpful and productive. My amazing friend Audrey is a great example of how these 2 things could come into play in figuring out how to value what we offer.

Audrey is super smart - and she works as a technical writer for a software company. We were talking about our strengths, and realized that we shared one that might explain a bit of why we enjoy talking with each other so much. We both love ideas, and are very good at taking a whole bunch of information, figuring out what is important, and how the ideas are related. We not only find ideas interesting in and of themselves, but see connections between ideas that other people don't seem to get until we explain it to them.

Audrey is a technical writer, creating documentation for software written by a lot of other people. She was telling me about she can connect the dots between actions in one part of the software, and how they will impact things in other parts of the software that even the people who are designing the software aren't really aware of. We had a long conversation about how she sees the implications of actions with respect to different parts of the software she's documenting, but something stood out for me. Audrey said, offhandedly, that at least she had job security.

Audrey is very well aware of the fact that what she offers her company as a technical writer has immense value, even though it's something she finds easier than - well, everyone else she knows of. In this case, I am guessing that it's partially because the effect is MEASUREABLE. When a client's system goes down, that's pretty concrete feedback that something isn't working. If you're the only one who knows what's going on and how to fix it? You are immensely valuable.

Contrast that technical skill with the talent for kindness. When you aren't as kind to a coworker as you could be, there's usually not an immediate, measurable impact on the company. But...maybe the next time you depend on that coworker, they aren't quite as quick to respond as they could be. The effect of your kindness (or lack of it!) is not so measurable, but it could still have a substantial overall impact on productivity and the company's bottom line. I could write a whole book on this, but there is also a lot of evidence that the effect of "soft skills", like how to communicate, and how to lead, are important but often not valued as much as skills that are easier to measure.

I feel that the effort required to manage relationships, especially relationships at work, are not given nearly enough credit. We are social creatures, and we are highly sensitive to issues about hierarchy, including the ways that hierarchy affects the availability of resources. In the environment in which we evolved, being aware of such things could literally mean the difference between life and death. I admit, there are issues with measuring soft skills, but I would argue that these soft skills are often presented in the form of talents.

If you identify with this paradox and would like some ways of figuring out ways around it, there are three main pieces that I see in the adventure of trying to best use your talents.

Identify Your Talents

First, you need to become aware of what your talents are. Our talents are often invisible to us - we find these things easy, and it can be a default to assume that everyone else does too. There are a lot of ways of figuring out your talents, including a lot of talent tests you can take. I found the Strengths Finder 2.0 a very useful tool - now it's called the CliftonStrenths talent test. If you're wondering what your talents are and want to take a test to find out, I highly recommend it.

Personally, my favourite way to get insight about your talents is to ask people who know you - you can get more information about why they associate you with a particular talent, and follow up. The possibilities for talents are also much larger than you will find with standard tests. It's also nice to hear what people appreciate about you! I was in a mastermind group, and at one of our last meetings we discussed what we had noticed about one another in terms of our strengths and how we presented ourselves. What stood out to one person about me is that I have a deep respect for other people. It was really nice to hear.

Looking back on my reaction to being told that my respect for people is something that stands out about me, I have to laugh. Even before I said anything I realized I had fallen into the Paradox of Talent. Yes, I do have a deep respect for other people, it's very important to me. I bring that respect into everything I do, and that's exactly why it stood out to someone. But my instinct was to say "But doesn't everyone?!" Even in that moment it was plain to me that I do a lot of the work that I do EXACTLY because other people don't have this talent. I spend time maintaining a level of respect for others at my events and in my groups. My reaction reinforced the fact for me that we often miss in ourselves those things that set us apart. We find our area of talent easy, and assume everyone else does too.

Discover How Your Talents Add Value

Second, after we see what sets us apart, we have to figure out how our talents provide value. Part of this adventure in understanding how you provide value is being open to taking compliments. Hear it and absorb it when people tell you something positive about yourself. Try not to downplay it, or brush it off. Keep in mind that by brushing off a compliment, you're also brushing off the other person's opinion. If someone says that you helped them, try simply saying "You're welcome" instead of something like "No problem." If someone tells you some way that you're awesome, just say "thank you." Many of us need to work on that.

Pay attention to how people are recognizing the value you offer.

One of the ways I spend a lot of my time is by leading my Facebook group Guelph Moms Supporting Moms. I run the group fairly differently than a lot of groups that I have seen, including my insistence that we can talk about difficult things, but need to do so in a way that respects all group members. I feel it's important to be able to talk about difficult things, both to get information and reduce shame, but sometimes these conversations get heated. We've talked about vaccines and inclusion relatively recently, and there were some comments that I didn't think were acceptable. I commented, both publicly and privately, and did my best to maintain a safe and respectful environment. Although sometimes conversations go off the rails, I deal with it, and one thing that has happened is that I have group members reach out to me afterward, usually with compliments about how I handled the situation, and how important the group is to them.

One thing I also keep hearing is that group members are very glad that I am running the group - that although it is very helpful for them, that they think I'm doing a great job and the group is better for my approach, they would never want to do what I do. My group members let me know that not only am I providing extreme value for them by running the group, it wouldn't be there without me. There's no one waiting in the wings to step up if for some reason I stop doing this work.

I'm needed.

Bring Your Talents to Work

Third, we need to figure out how to incorporate our talents into our work. Now, if your version of being a pear tree is being a world class accountant or computer programmer, this might not be a huge issue for you. But for many of us, our best talents are things that are a little harder to put into a traditional career.

One strategy is to simply do more of what you're good at in your work. In my career as a consultant on a team, I did a project presentation for a client even though traditionally it would have been the project leader who would do that. She doesn't like giving presentations, and I do and am good at it, so we switched up the task assignments. If you have a boss who will be flexible about who does what, it makes sense to become clear about the talents of team members and to assign tasks accordingly.

Another strategy of course would be to find what your strength is and find a job that uses more of your talents. It takes a lot of work sometimes to find an ideal job, especially when your talent is something like respecting people. You might want to try exploring different hobbies or volunteer work to see if something starts feeling like it's using your talents.

You might also find that your ideal work, work that uses your talents, starts to find YOU. I struggled to find something meaningful to do when I started my entrepreneurial journey - I knew that I wanted to help moms (and through them their kids), but I didn't really know how to best accomplish that. Then a few months later I got the opportunity to start my Facebook group. It seemed like a great opportunity to support and make contact with local moms, so I jumped in. Leading my Facebook group has not only helped me do the work that I wanted to do, but it has also been a huge learning opportunity to find out my talents and how they add value. Since then, I've also become a confidence trainer as well as a community builder, and my strengths in respecting people and their emotions are invaluable in those roles.

You May Not WANT Your Talent

One thing to keep in mind though, is that just because you're talented at something doesn't mean you necessarily WANT to do it. It is sort of a default to assume that people love doing what they're great at, but that's not always the case. I have a good friend named Rachel who is great at organizing. She's so amazing at it that in most jobs she's had, she has ended up in some role in which she's responsible for a lot of organizing.

She hates it.

It's totally reasonable to avoid doing something you're good at if you don't like it. It's also a possibility that you do enjoy what you're talented at, but you want to keep it a part time thing, or a hobby. Maybe you're an awesome programmer, but you'd rather program some games in your free time, and keep your plumbing job as your "regular" job. I remember the first time I was paid to crochet a blanket - crochet was something I loved as a hobby, but the pressure to do a paid project took a lot of the fun out of the process for me.

Five Growing Questions about Talent:

1. Name three of your talents. If you can't, then ask your friends to describe your talents, or take a talent test.

2. How do your talents add value to the world?

3. What is a way you really enjoy using one of your talents? What's a way you don't like using one of your talents?

4. Do you know someone who downplays their talent? Write a letter to them describing how you see their talent and the value that it offers. Consider sharing the letter with them.

5. When someone thanks you for something or compliments you about something, how do you respond? If you're

dismissive of your work or talents, consider simply saying "thank you" or "you're welcome". How does that feel?

Talent Summary Question:

What was one thing you learned in this chapter about talent that you want to include in your personal definition of success? Write or dictate a note for yourself, or put it in the appropriate section of the journal provided (find out how to download the journal for free at http://tamsen.ca/paradoxjournalfree).

> Whatever makes you different or weird - that's your strength.
>
> - Meryl Streep

Curiosity #13 - The Balance Myth

Balance is a feeling derived from being whole and complete; it's a sense of harmony. It is essential to maintaining quality in life and work.

- Joshua Osenga

I was honoured to be a part of a discussion about leadership and vulnerability for a segment of the C-Suite, a local tv show hosted by my friend Danielle Joworski (you can watch it here - http: / / tamsen.ca / csuite). I stuck around after my segment, and the last filmed segment was about the notorious "work life balance". Living a "balanced life" is often held up as a sign of success, something to aspire to. But a main aspect of the segment was a discussion of whether work life balance can even exist (you can watch it here - http://tamsen.ca/csuitebalance).

The two women being interviewed about how to create a balanced life had some good points about overwhelm, and how to use certain tools like colour coded calendars to make sure that you had a good overview of your schedule and how you were spending your time. There was an interesting discussion of changing the term "work-life balance" to "work-life integration". Most people benefit from having flexibility in their work schedules, and being able to shift work commitments around to accommodate real life tasks like dentist appointments, or even self care like spa appointments.

Two things struck me about this conversation.

Motherhood Fills Your Plate - and Changes Who You Are

First, although both women were successful and had many valuable points to offer and many things to juggle in their lives, neither had children. Motherhood not only puts a whole other full time job (or more!) worth of tasks on our plate, but also brings in a lot of stuff about responsibilities, priorities, judgement, identity, and probably a lot of other ideas that need exploring to really understand what balance and a successful life are for many of us.

Balance is a FEELING

The second thing that struck me is that there is a huge emotional component to this conversation that largely got ignored. When people talk about feeling successful, being out of overwhelm and anxiety, finding balance, it's a feeling they're talking about. But this emotional experience generally gets translated into the thinking experience of knowing that you got things done at the end of the day, or the action of being able to check off all the items on your "to do" list.

After thinking about this for a few days, I realized that I see work life balance as a particular type of confidence - what I define as a sense of trust and safety. I think that a feeling of work life balance is the confidence that you are doing the right thing at the right time, based on your priorities, goals, and values. That is balance and part of a successful life.

That's the Balance Myth - Balance isn't about getting everything done. Balance is the feeling of confidence we get when we connect with our values and priorities so we can choose to do the right thing at the right time.

Balance Isn't that Things Go as Planned

It may sound a bit strange, but the time I remember feeling the most balanced was one day when the whole morning went sideways and I chose to do something that I hadn't planned.

My son has been sick with some sort of virus that turned into bronchitis which then turned into pneumonia. I wasn't feeling particularly balanced after spending most of 2 weeks home with him, especially since I had gotten sick too! There were certain things I felt I needed to do, both for my business and general well-being, that just weren't happening. So, I was way more excited than my son when the doctor gave him the all clear to go back to school. We showed up and Tommy's best friend run up to him, so excited that he had made it back - because today was the day their class was doing their Christmas play! My son was totally overwhelmed - he was surprised, didn't feel prepared, was afraid to be on stage - and when he heard that the play included the Grinch, that was the last straw.

Crap.

We hustled inside to talk to his teacher about what he could do instead of participating in the play - she offered to have him sit with her, but the idea of being with her even offstage didn't soothe my son. So Tommy and I went and sat in the audience, and watched the play together. We talked about Minecraft™ - that's what Tommy wanted to do to calm down. And even the Grinch wasn't so bad (it got a thumbs sideways instead of a thumbs down. Progress!)

What I was "supposed" to be doing, what was my plan? I would drop off my son at school, and go off to a networking breakfast. I was looking forward to seeing some friends, getting some adult social time, and starting to feel like things were back on track. Then I'd spend the rest of the morning catching up on some actual work! But as my son huddled into me, as we talked, as I watched him calm down and then go to class without complaint after the play was over, I had that feeling of being balanced, grounded. I was exactly where I needed to be, where I wanted to be, doing what I wanted to be doing - in that moment, for that hour. Despite my plans, despite anything else going on.

I felt immense peace.

So how to get to balanced?

Since you can't do everything, how do you decide what to do? Especially if everything is hitting the fan and you need to choose between a bunch of things that all feel important?

One of the most important questions to ask is - what can you let go and pick up later without damage?

Can You Drop this Ball?

So, we're facing it - we can't expect to be able to do everything.

Here's a useful question that might help you decide what to choose - is the thing you're thinking of dropping - like a ball - is it rubber or is it glass? I mean - if you have to let something go, will it bounce, so you can pick it up again? Or will it shatter and be gone or badly damaged? When you're trying to make a decision about what to let go - are there things you're juggling that you can put aside for awhile, and pick up later? Deadlines that can be pushed, meetings that can be rescheduled, laundry that can remain unfolded?

I work with a lot of moms, and we understand each other when plans have to be changed because our kids need us. I want to work with moms who would take the time to be there for their kids when needed, and who respect that I will do the same. So these plans are like rubber balls - if either of us can't juggle it right now, it will bounce, and we can pick it up again at a time that works for both of us. On the other hand - if my son needs me and I say no? That feels like a glass ball.

Balance Comes from Knowing Your Values, Goals, and Priorities

Letting things go responsibly takes some management. Just not showing up to a meeting when you're expected isn't responsible if you can let people know in advance. But building in the ability to make as many of the things you're juggling into rubber balls pays off! If you've taken the time to really dig into your values, you may already have one or two guiding values to help you make decisions about what to let go when you have to make that choice. If you haven't, I'll be guiding you through that exercise in the Redefining Success section.

Mindfulness and self-compassion can also help a great deal here. No matter the importance of what we're doing, sometimes it's difficult to stop thinking about what we're not doing and bashing ourselves for it. We have to remind ourselves that we're humans with limited time and resources, and give the myth of the superwoman a rest.

Of course, feel free to disagree with me - and when you do, I'd love to hear about what balance is for you! When do you feel balanced (or off balance) the most? Send me your insights at tamsen@tamsenconnects.com!

Five Growing Questions about Balance:

1. Have you ever really thought about what your top values are? If so, list them. If not, take some time to do that now.

2. Is there a decision that you're currently struggling with? Would being clearer about your values help you make that decision?

3. Is there a decision you made in the past that you regret? What did it teach you about your values and priorities?

4. Is there a difficult decision you made in the past that you're happy with? What did it teach you about your values and priorities?

5. To what extent do you prioritize work or other "balls" that could bounce and be picked up later, over ones that are glass and could shatter like your relationships or your health? What comes up for you about this choice?

Balance Summary Question:

What was one thing you learned in this chapter about balance that you want to include in your personal definition of success? Write or dictate a note for yourself, or put it in the appropriate section of the journal provided (find out how to download the journal for free at http://tamsen.ca/paradoxjournalfree).

> Work is a rubber ball. If you drop it, it will bounce back. The other four balls - family, health, friends, and integrity - are made of glass. If you drop one of these, it will be irrevocably scuffed, nicked, perhaps even shattered.
>
> - Gary Keller

Curiosity #14 - The Paradox of Options

Learning to choose is hard. Learning to choose well is harder. And learning to choose well in a world of unlimited possibilities is harder still, perhaps too hard.

- Barry Schwartz

I have a favourite restaurant - it's a Vietnamese-Thai place called Ben Thanh. I often suggest we go to Ben Thanh when my friends want to meet for lunch - the food is amazing, and it's a relatively inexpensive place. Another notable thing about this restaurant is the HUGE menu. Funny thing is, even with the very large menu, I usually order the same thing every time I go. And for my friends or acquaintances who haven't been there before, ordering a meal can turn into an ordeal. Often it just turns into "what's good?!", and then once the food has arrived, they look around, commenting on the food on other tables, wondering what else might be better than what they ordered.

> That's the paradox of options - having more options is supposed to result in a better outcome, but **if we have a lot of options that often leads to getting stuck, being less satisfied, and feeling unsuccessful**.

Of course, this huge array of options causing us to get stuck is a relatively minor problem when it comes to choosing a meal - darn it, we might have had something a bit better - eat our dinner, move on. Maybe make a mental note of what to try next time! The problem is, this abundance of choice can have negative effects for more important decisions, like career options, that directly impact how successful we feel.

I remember my mom saying that "In her day", she had 4 choices of what to be. She could be a nurse, a teacher, a secretary, or a stay at home wife and mother. Sounds limiting, sure. But at the same time, I remember considering going to university. What could I be? Pretty much anything. How hard was it to choose not only where to go, but what to study? It was excruciating and nerve wracking! What if I made the "wrong" choice? To be honest, I did make a wrong choice for me and went into chemistry (I lasted a couple of years before switching to psychology). And now? I'm an entrepreneur, which means I can do absolutely anything and create my own work.

Having an abundance of options sounds good, but there are two main problems it creates on our path to building a successful life.

Problem #1 - Too Many Options Results in Analysis Paralysis

First, when you have a lot of options it can be too overwhelming to choose, and so you get stuck.

This "analysis paralysis" is one reason when you're trying to help a toddler get dressed you don't let them stand in front of their closet and choose from all possible options. You choose 2 acceptable outfits, let them choose the red one or the blue one, then you can move on with your day. Otherwise, if you give the toddler access to all of the options in their closet, they end up like someone anxious about a first date. They're mostly naked with the entire wardrobe of clothes spread over the room and can't make up their mind which outfit is EXACTLY right. Either that or they want the one that's in the dirty laundry!

Problem #2 - You Missed the "Perfect" Option

When you have a lot of options, doesn't it seem like you should be able to find the PERFECT outfit (or the perfect partner, career, holiday, whatever)?

Here's the truth - Even if you make the exact best choice for you out of all possible options, you're still going to have all your feelings, and you're still going to have bad days. But now, since you could have chosen something else, you tend to blame yourself for choosing the wrong thing rather than just accepting that there are good and bad things about any choice that you could have made, and working your way through the difficult feelings and bad days without kicking yourself for it.

Tips for Making Decisions with Lots of Options

We've discussed why it can be really hard to make decisions when you have lots of options. Here are some suggestions for how to get unstuck!

Tip #1 - Be Aware

Simply being aware of the tendency to get stuck when you have too many options can be freeing. Practice some compassion for yourself and realize this is a common reaction.

Tip #2 - Break Decisions into Pieces

Sometimes breaking down a decision into parts can also help. If you're trying to decide where to go on vacation, rather than comparing resorts in multiple countries, can you decide the country you want to go to first, then look at places to stay to narrow down your options?

Tip #3 - Collaborate

Is there someone else affected by the decision who can help you narrow options down? Maybe they have strong opinions about the decision, or a different perspective that can make the number of acceptable options seem more reasonable. You can also talk to people who have had to make a similar decision to see if they have any suggestions.

Tip #4 - Stop Maximizing and Start Satisficing

One major strategy for making decisions when you have lots of options is to accept that you won't be able to find a perfect answer, and finding a choice that is a little bit better might take more time and energy than you want to spend on the decision.

My husband and I had to replace our dishwasher a few years ago. To say the least, we have different styles of making decisions. He's a hard core, get the right data, Consumer Reports kind of guy. He's a "Maximizer". He needed to find THE BEST

CHOICE! I let him go to it, I didn't really have strong feelings about what kind of dishwasher to get, I just wanted one ASAP.

Unfortunately, he got stuck. The Consumer Reports data he could get was based on the U.S., and the model numbers available in Canada didn't match up. It wasn't a simple thing to translate, every single brand had multiple models, and it was very difficult to tell the ones that got good reviews from the ones that were getting bad reviews. So I went online, looked at a few popular dishwashers, and picked 2 I thought I would be happy with, and told him to choose from those. At least for this decision, I was a "Satisficer".

We got a dishwasher - and it's been ok. But one of the things I hate about it isn't something that I even thought to consider when I was making the decision! Our dishes don't fit properly in the bottom rack, and certain bowls use up way too much space. I point out this example because when we are trying to make a decision, often we don't consider everything that could impact how happy we are with our decision later. We often don't know what that's going to be!

Take a pass on Maximizing. Recognize when good enough is good enough.

Tip #5 - Recognize that Most Decisions Aren't Forever

Remember that decisions usually don't have to be forever if you really found you chose badly. Often when we're faced with big decisions, especially in relationships, it seems like you have to choose a path and commit to it forever. If I was willing to spend the money I could replace our dishwasher, so I'm choosing to live with the fact it's not ideal. You can change careers, even if it might seem scary. You can go back to school, even if you're one of the older ones in your class. And I don't need to remind you that even marriage isn't forever these days.

I want to mention that one of the main sources of inspiration for this chapter is the work by Barry Schwartz - check out his TED talk, it's amazing.

Five Growing Questions about Options:

1. Do you struggle when you have a lot of options to choose from? Do you have ways of dealing with this struggle?

2. Do you identify as a "maximizer", a "satisficer", or neither? Does the importance of the decision influence that?

3. Whether or not you are one, what is the most helpful thing about being a maximizer? The least helpful?

4. Whether or not you are one, what is the most helpful thing about being a satisficer? The least helpful?

5. You will have good days and bad days, no matter what your decision. Do you find that helpful or depressing? Why?

Options Summary Question:

What was one thing you learned in this chapter about options that you want to include in your personal definition of success? Write or dictate a note for yourself, or put it in the appropriate section of the journal provided (find out how to download the journal for free at http://tamsen.ca/paradoxjournalfree).

In any moment of decision, the best thing you can do is the right thing. The worst thing you can do is nothing.

- Theodore Roosevelt

Curiosity #15 - The Paradox of Fear

Try a thing you haven't done three times. Once, to get over the fear of doing it. Twice, to learn how to do it. And a third time to figure out whether you like it or not.

- Virgil Thomson

Sooo.... What are you afraid of?

Fear is an emotion that puts us on alert, that makes us aware of potential danger in our environment. We pay more attention to what's going on. It's important to remember that fear can literally mean the difference between life and death.

Our fears are influenced by a lot of things, not least by the hardwiring we have from evolution. In our current world, car accidents are way more likely to harm us than spiders or snakes, but we don't seem as likely to develop phobias about being around cars! So phobias can make fear seem overblown and unhelpful.

Do you have any phobias? Fears that are out of proportion to the real danger? Mine is spiders (*shudder*).

So sometimes fear saves our lives, and sometimes its main effect is to make our lives uncomfortable - even miserable.

To add to this confusion about whether fear is valuable or worse than useless, often we're told that fear is what is holding us back from success. We're supposed to "feel the fear and do it anyway" if we are struggling to build a life where we feel successful.

> That's the paradox of fear - we're told to "feel the fear and do it anyway" for success, but fear is valuable information, and it's there for a reason. **How can we tell when we should ignore our fears and when we should listen to them?**

Practice Lessens Fear… Except When it Doesn't

I had a very interesting interview with Mary Strachan for my Momtellectual podcast about the nature of fear, and when we should listen to it versus ignore it. My favourite insight Mary shared was that if you do something you're afraid of, often it will get easier after you do it a few times. Practice helps us feel more comfortable and so our fear lessens. Practice also helps us get better. We talked about this in Curiosity #4 - The Confidence Myth. But sometimes practice doesn't make something less scary (and we're not talking about cliff jumping here!) You can find Mary's episode of Momtellectual, Fear is a Clue, here - tamsen.ca/momtellectual65.

Mary's example of a time she had to deal with fear was doing business reachouts to build her business and make it more successful. Many entrepreneurs hate some aspect of doing marketing and sales calls. Most will admit that fear plays a part in that. We hate to feel rejected, we hate to hear "no". We worry that we're being annoying. But going through and following a plan, whether it's calling people on the phone, emailing them, whatever, after the first few times it should start to feel easier.

What if practice doesn't make something easier?

One thing to consider is whether what you're doing is consistent with your values. Mary suggests that if something doesn't get easier and your fear get less after you do something a few times, that's a strong sign that you probably shouldn't be doing that thing, or doing it in that way. We'll be digging deeper into identifying your values in the Redefining Success section.

For now, keep in mind that truly feeling successful depends not only on WHAT you're doing, but HOW you do it.

There's a lot of research that our decisions aren't really ruled by logic, but that being able to make decisions at all is largely an emotional process. Antonio Damasio's book Descartes' Error: Emotion, Reason, and the Human Brain is a very readable example of this research. One of the reasons that I think this is true is that taking our values, goals, and priorities into account is probably done through our emotions, rather than as a painstaking, conscious process. If multiple values come into conflict, logically it's often unclear which of our values should "win". Also, I've found that the way we interpret a value can be very different from person to person. Have you heard someone say they value family, and by that they mean they spend a lot of time with their kids? Someone else says they value family, and what they mean by that is they hardly see their children at all, because they're so busy at work trying to earn money so they can afford to feed and clothe their kids (or maybe put money aside for school).

So, an initial feeling of fear might be a fear of doing something new, but if it doesn't go away with practice then maybe it's about doing something that goes against your core values.

Dangers Changed, but Fear Didn't

It's true that our emotions are geared toward an environment like we evolved in, and not like we live in now. This mismatch between our current circumstances and the situations in which we evolved can cause a similar mismatch between what our emotions want to tell us and what information would be useful.

Read Curiosity #10 - the Paradox of Loneliness for a specific example. We evolved to like sweet and salty things in an environment where they were hard to find, and there wasn't a fast food joint on every corner. Now there IS a fast food joint on every corner, and our craving for sweet and salty things results in obesity and lots of health issues. In the same way, we evolved to fear rejection, because if we were tossed out of our core group of people, we would die. Usually rejection doesn't have such severe consequences these days.

When we're afraid to do something, people sometimes ask us "well, what's the worst that could happen?" If you can accept that the actual consequences NOW aren't really bad, then it's a signal that our fear is likely rooted in how bad the consequences USED to be. Making some peace with the fact that we carry hardwiring that sometimes isn't helpful now can be a first step toward doing the things that we need to do to do our best work and live our best lives.

Five Growing Questions about Fear:

1. Is there something you're afraid of doing right now that you feel you "should" do? Do you think the fear is there because it's something new, or something that goes against your values?

2. Are you afraid of being rejected? Does it surprise you that this fear likely comes from our evolutionary past? Does that knowledge help you be less afraid of rejection?

3. When do you believe it's helpful to face our fears and do something even though we're afraid?

4. When do you believe it's helpful to listen to our fears and not do something we're afraid of?

5. Have you ever chosen to not listen to a fear of yours and regretted it? What did that experience teach you?

Fear Summary Question:

What was one thing you learned in this chapter about fear that you want to include in your personal definition of success? Write or dictate a note for yourself, or put it in the appropriate section of the journal provided (find out how to download the journal for free at http://tamsen.ca/paradoxjournalfree).

> You must never be fearful about what you are doing when it is right.
>
> - Rosa Parks

Creating Meaning: Summary

Your passion is waiting for your courage to catch up.

- Isabelle Lafleche

The Creating Meaning section is about connecting with your passions and sense of purpose. In this summary section, we're checking back in to see what's changed with the new insights you have gained.

You may be able to answer these questions right away. You may also want to reexamine your answers to the review questions from each chapter in this section, and decide on which feels the most important to include in your personal definition of success right now.

Remember that there is no "right" or "wrong" answer. If you're having trouble deciding, don't stress about it. There will be time to decide what to focus on when you're deciding on your action plan - and I'll introduce some strategies to help you deal with overwhelm if you're still having trouble deciding then!

Review Questions:

Check in - has reading this section and answering the questions changed any of your answers?

1. Definition question: What does it mean to have a "meaningful life" to you right now, after reading this section?

2. Self-assessment question: What is the current level of meaning in your life right now, after reading this section?

3. Goal question: What is the main thing you want to change about the level of meaning you have in your life right now, after reading this section?

4. Achievement question: How will you know you've achieved your level of meaning goal?

You can't have everything you want, but you can have the things that really matter to you.

- Marissa Mayer

Section: Redefining Success

Success is liking yourself, liking what you do, and liking how you do it.

- Maya Angelou

A fundamental belief underlying the ideas presented in this book is that success isn't one thing for everyone, or even a "one and done" thing for ANYONE.

Success is something that is connected to needs that most of us share - so we will discuss these "universal" needs. It's also important to recognize how success is also deeply PERSONAL. This book is a tool to guide you in creating your own personal definition of success. It's important to create that personal definition of success based on things that are in your power to control, and to create that definition of success something that you can experience NOW, rather than some vague point in the future.

I want feeling successful right now to be the gift you give yourself by doing this work.

Let's move our journey from being curious to DOING.

What is Success?

I love that Maya Angelou quote about success - I used it to guide my first virtual summit, about how to be a successful mother. I guess I would also add - success is also liking who you do it with. And those topics fit fairly well into the topics we've discussed in this book (Creating Self-Worth, Creating Healthy Relationships, and Creating Meaning). Yet, let's dig deeper, and discuss several things that influence our search for success.

Know it's possible to create a life you want to live.

Sophie Milliken's story is a great example - in her words, she started from less than zero. As a newly divorced mom of a young daughter, she had a ton of debt and lots of responsibility! She was driven to start her own company primarily because she wanted to have the flexibility to be the parent she wanted to be. Now Sophie is Managing Director of her educational consulting firm SRS, author of the best selling book "From Learner to Earner", and just before our Momtellectual podcast interview she presented an invited TED talk. Sophie shares her story to provide hope, to let other women know that success is often a difficult journey, and to point out that success usually looks way easier from the outside than from the inside. (Starting Over, Momtellectual Episode 140 - you can find it at tamsen.ca/momtellectual140).

Redefining Success Orienting Questions:

1. Definition question: What does "success" mean to you right now?

2. Self-assessment question: What is your current level of success?

3. Goal question: What is the main thing you want to change about your level of success?

4. Achievement question: How will you know you've achieved your success goal?

The key is not to prioritize what's on your schedule, but to schedule your priorities.

- Stephen Covey

Understand Universal Needs

We often don't know what we actually want. Even if there's a first, fast answer, the question 'But what do you really want?' will typically stop people in their tracks.

- Michael Bungay Stanier

It's important to define success for ourselves, but in beginning that process it is beneficial to consider needs that have been scientifically identified as nearly universal, to make sure that we figure out if we need them and incorporate them in our definition of success if necessary.

Truth Bomb - You Need to Know What you Want

What do you want? It sounds like a simple question.

As noted by Michael Bungay Stanier in his amazing book "The Coaching Habit", it's important yet difficult to identify what you really want. He discusses why it's important to separate wants and needs, and how wants can be a clue to needs by looking at wants and figuring out what needs are driving them. So, if you think you know what you want - what is it? Then see what universal need might underlie that want. It might help you be even more clear about what you really want.

If you're not sure what you want, check and see how you're doing with the universal needs, and check that you have them all covered. If not, that might be a clue about how you need to change your life to feel successful.

Here is one list of such "universal" needs, according to the Center for Nonviolent Communication (https://www.cnvc.org/). To refer to this appropriately they ask anyone to share this:

(c) 2005 by Center for Nonviolent Communication
Website: www.cnvc.org
Email: cnvc@cnvc.org
Phone: +1.505-244-4041

Each of these needs are described by the needs that fall into those categories, so I'm including a few of those. If you'd like to see everything that's included, definitely check out the reference link for the Center for Nonviolent Communication that I've included.

Connection: The need for connection includes ideas like the need for acceptance, appreciation, community, empathy, inclusion, love, and nurturing. Safety and trust also fall into this need.

Physical Well-Being: This category includes the needs related to basic physical survival, like air, food, exercise, sleep, shelter, water, and (yes) touch.

Honesty: The need for honesty includes the need fort things like authenticity, integrity, and presence.

Play: this category includes joy and humour.

Peace: The need for peace includes the appreciation of beauty, communion, ease, equality, harmony, inspiration, and order.

Autonomy: The need for autonomy includes the need for things like choice, freedom, independence, space, and spontaneity.

Meaning: this category of needs includes the need for awareness, celebration of life, clarity, competence, consciousness, creativity, discovery, growth, hope, learning, participation, purpose, self-expression, understanding.

So, where do you stand on meeting these universal needs? Do you feel you have a need that isn't listed? That could very well be - the above list isn't definitive.

Now that you have a clearer idea of what you want and need, it's time to make it happen.

Five Growing Questions about What you Want:

1. So… What do you really want?

2. What is a part of your life that you're really satisfied with? Could you expand that in your life?

3. Which of the universal needs are currently being met in your life (connection, physical well-being, honesty, play, peace, autonomy, meaning)?

4. Which of the universal needs are NOT currently being met in your life (connection, physical well-being, honesty, play, peace, autonomy, meaning)?

5. If all of your needs were being met, how would that change your life?

What Do You Want Summary Question:

What was one thing you learned about what you want that you want to include in your personal definition of success? Write or dictate a note for yourself, or put it in the appropriate section of the journal provided (find out how to download the journal for free at http://tamsen.ca/paradoxjournalfree).

If I had known what it would be like to have it all - I might have been willing to settle for less.

- Lily Tomlin

Redefine Success: Make Success Personal

It's not hard to make decisions when you know what your values are.

- Roy Disney

Some parts of success that are worth examining are close to universal. Universal needs are the beginning, not the end. In this chapter we'll discuss some ways to make your definition of success personal to you.

When someone works with me one on one to address their confidence challenges, I ask them to fill out two questionnaires to get a handle on their love languages and some insights into their personality (I usually suggest three quizzes, but the third quiz we'll discuss in the What to do if You're Still Struggling to Feel Successful chapter coming up later). These tests aren't foolproof, but they're currently free, and do offer some interesting insights. Whenever I talk to someone about redefining success, most people also benefit from looking deeply at their values and priorities, to make sure that their effort is likely to be rewarded.

Let's look at these!

The 16 Personalities Quiz

You can find the free test here - tamsen.ca/16personalities

Using myself as an example, I'll share some things I learned, and some things that might be helpful for you to look at specifically. Of course, if you want to read the whole thing that's great too!

I'm a Campaigner - an ENFP. Those letters won't mean much to you unless you know the underlying dimensions to this test. You can read more about them from the original site at https://www.16personalities.com/articles/our-theory

The dimensions are interesting, but for our purposes, I'd like to dig more into the profiles provided by this test.

Here are 2 goals that I suggest you have as you read your profile:

You may get genuine AH HAs!!! Those things that shed light on your personality in ways that you really hadn't realized before. These tests show you how you are different from other people, and sometimes take the filter off your perspective and let you see things in a new way. In my case, when I read "Few things matter more to these personality types [Campaigners] than having genuine, heartfelt conversations with the people they cherish." - I definitely connected with this. It clarified for me that I not only need "social time" - but if that social time is superficial, with people I don't really care about, it will never satisfy me the same way that meaningful, helpful conversations with my dear friends will.

Sometimes you get told something you knew, but would have difficult communicating. It's possible that the best value of tests like these are that they tell us things that we already knew, but emphasize their benefits and give us clearer ways to communicate about our value. For me, it helps to have the language that "Campaigners are proof that seeking out life's joys and pleasures isn't the same as being shallow." Fun is one of my top 5 values - yet to some people, that can seem really superficial. Yet fun and joy is one of the best ways to connect to our joy, our passions, and through those to our deepest purpose and meaning.

I also want to emphasize - as someone who in teaching undergraduate classes always rejoiced when I could find an error in a textbook to show that you shouldn't always just trust what you read, even in a textbook - don't just accept that something you read in this or any test is right for you. As an example, where I depart from accepting the Campaigner personality type as mine, there is this quote: "Campaigners may end up puzzling over someone else's desires or intentions. This kind of social stress is what keeps harmony-focused Campaigners awake at night."

Nope.

I definitely spend time thinking about other people's desires and intentions - but I am NOT harmony-focused. I am way more disharmony focused! Harmony can sound good - put simply, it's the desire for everyone to agree and get along. But I genuinely am more excited and interested when people disagree - although it's a boundary for me that everyone treat each other with respect. If everyone agrees life is really boring. I much prefer engaging in conversations with people with differing perspectives, and if we can engage with each other with genuine curiosity and respect, we have the chance of getting information we wouldn't get otherwise. I really value that.

So, please do take this and any quiz result with a grain of salt. Don't automatically assume what it tells you is true or helpful - please allow yourself to question and decide for yourself.

The Love Languages Quiz

You can find the free test here - tamsen.ca/lovelanguages

There are five main love languages - acts of service, words of affirmation, physical touch, gifts, and quality time.

The love language research was originally created in the context of marriage counselling. In trying to help married couples communicate, its creator Gary Chapman realized that not everyone communicates about love the same way. Understanding how the other person in our relationship communicates about love can be key in resolving disputes and helping each person FEEL loved.

Here are my recommendations for using the results of this test so they are most helpful:

Take the test for yourself - use it to help you understand your own "hot buttons" aka what really pisses you off in your relationships, and also help you understand what to ask for in your relationships so you can really feel loved.

Ask the people in your relationships to take this test so you can understand best how to communicate your love to them.

If people in your life won't take the test, you can follow the guides to understand how to best guess their main love language.

Consider that sometimes how people want to receive love and how they want to give love can be different.

Consider that, especially with kids moving into the teen years, their love language can stay the same, but the actual interaction can change. Your young child may love hugs, but then your teen might prefer high 5's. Both are physical touch, but the type of touch changes.

One of the most valuable things this test can tell you is YOUR love language - and give you clues about when you don't feel loved. It can also show you that it might not be appropriate to insist that you get love the way YOU want, if your loved one doesn't want to interact that way.

Know Your Values

Understanding your values can really help make decision making easier.

When my friend Susan Gentilcore had her first business it was a storefront. She remembers people would come in with questions, comments or demands that you'd never think of until it happened. She had a business partner at the time, and there were problems with having a united front when people came in with requests or complaints. The strategy that Susan and her parter adopted was to decide what their boundaries were for all sorts of different things. They developed completely unwritten "store policies" - so when people came in and asked for any random demand, they could quote a store policy.

Susan mentioned that every so often someone would call us out and say "But YOU'RE the owner!" She and her parter could reply "Yes, and we've developed these store policies." Because there were two of them as partners, they developed store policies so they were on the same page. Without those store policies, it was likely that they'd both get trampled, pushed in a bunch of different directions that didn't make sense, and didn't make either of them comfortable. Knowing those principles and being able to remove the guilt for not being able to meet everyone else's needs helped both Susan and her business parter meet their own needs.

Creating something like Susan and her business partner's store policies is much easier when you can identify your core values. It can be a challenging process to narrow your core values down to just 1 or 2 - but when you take the time to do that, you will create for yourself a guide that can really clarify which choices are right for you. This is especially critical when you need to make decisions quickly.

Why 1 or 2 Values Max?

Brené Brown talks about this process, and I agree with her - if you try to focus on more than 2 values, things get muddy really quickly. If you value a lot of things "the most", then the effect is essentially that you value nothing. It doesn't help you make decisions and doesn't act as a useful guide.

I highly recommend you take the time to do this activity, even if it takes you awhile.

I'm including a list of 50 popular values here as a starting point - most people have huge difficulty in narrowing down this list to their 1 or 2 top values. If you have the opposite problem and you just don't feel that your top value is in that list, you can visit a longer list on my blog at https://www.tamsenconnects.com/post/values-list. If you'd like a printable pdf of the following list, you can download one at https://www.tamsenconnects.com/post/values-list-shorter. After the list, there are some questions to help you if you're still struggling to narrow down the list to your top 1 or 2 values.

Values List:

Achievement
Beauty
Cleanliness
Comfort
Compassion
Competition
Control
Courage
Creativity
Dependability
Empathy
Excellence
Fame
Family
Freedom
Gratitude
Happiness
Health
Honesty
Hope
Independence
Integrity
Intelligence
Intuition
Justice
Kindness
Love
Minimalism
Nature
Passion
Patience
Peace
Personal Growth
Piety
Play
Poise
Potential
Power
Predictability
Prosperity
Purity
Rebellion
Relationships
Respect
Service
Spirituality
Sustainability
Time
Tolerance
Tradition

If You're Still Struggling to Narrow Down the List:

- Are there any values still on the list because you feel you "should" value them, but they're not really the most important thing? It can be really hard to cross off values like "family" without feeling guilty. I challenge you to do it anyway! You don't have to share this list with anyone.

- What do you think the world really needs more of? If you could wave a magic wand and increase one of these things for everyone, what would make the biggest positive difference in the world?

- What value would you like to be known for?

- Are you unsure about your top value because you sometimes struggle with it? Valuing something highly doesn't mean that it's always easy for you.

- My friend Shanan had another suggestion - remember the last interaction you had with someone that felt "wrong". Can you identify a value that was violated? That is likely to be a value that's really important to you.

Five Growing Questions about Making Success Personal:

1. What is your 16 personalities type? What were some "Ah-has" you got from reading it?

2. Did your 16 personalities type description give you a better idea of how to describe your personality and the value you offer? Where can you use this?

3. What is your love language profile? Does that tell you why you really feel loved sometimes, and why you feel unloved at other times?

4. Did exploring the different Love Language types give you any insights about how to show love to other people in your life?

5. What are your two core values? Can you rank them? Spend some time journalling about what these values mean to you, and why you feel they're important.

Making Success Personal Summary Question:

What was one thing you learned in this chapter about Making success personal that you want to include in your personal definition of success? Write or dictate a note for yourself, or put it in the appropriate section of the journal provided (find out how to download the journal for free at http://tamsen.ca/paradoxjournalfree).

> For me, I am driven by two main philosophies: know more today about the world than I knew yesterday and lessen the suffering of others. You'd be surprised how far that gets you.
>
> - Neil deGrasse Tyson

Redefine Success: Make Success in Your Control

> Incredible change happens in your life when you decide to take control of what you do have power over instead of craving control over what you don't.
>
> - Steve Maraboli

You can't control everything. Arguably, we can't control most things. But creating a definition of success that isn't really in your control won't be the most helpful to you. So let's address the Control Myth.

The Control Myth

My life is predictably unpredictable.

I have a son who is sick a lot, and who often needs time and attention from me. Part of the redemption that I have found in a life that is unpredictable is that I have been working hard to become more comfortable with that unpredictability. I see people trying to control things and predict things all around me, and I try to leave them to it because they usually need to do that to feel safe. Taking predictability away when they're not ready isn't really going to be helpful. But for me, working to accept and embrace the fact that life is inherently unpredictable is one of the ways that I have lowered my stress. I can make plans but make sure that I can contact people if I need to reschedule a meeting at the last minute, so I don't feel inconsiderate and unprofessional. Instead of saying "I have to stay home with my son today", I can say "I get to stay home with my son today", and try to have some fun with him!

There are all sorts of productivity and success hacks, tips, and coaches out there. There are all sorts of planning tools and schedules, and ways to organize your life. There are also all sorts of reminders that change can come at unpredictable times, and we often build up expectations that don't come to pass. For many of us, the pandemic really hit us hard with the unpredictability of life. I had a great interview with Marisa Raymond for my Momtellectual podcast that was recorded right at the beginning of the pandemic. Marisa and I discussed the huge uncertainty that the pandemic brought, and the difficulty that comes with feeling a lack of control. (Momtellectual episode 118, Pandemic Parenting. Find it at tamsen.ca/momtellectual118).

I don't think there is any way for most of us to not have expectations - but we can cultivate an openness to things being different than we expect.

Control Through Self-Blame

Miscarriage is common. Statistically, as many as 1 in 4 known pregnancies end in miscarriage, and if you consider that often miscarriages can appear to be a late period, miscarriages might occur much more frequently than 1 in 4. Of course, miscarriage being common doesn't make it easy. I've spoken with a lot of women who have suffered the loss of a child through miscarriage. Having a child die, even if we only got to be pregnant with them for a short time, is extremely difficult for many women.

One of the very challenging things about miscarriage is that often we don't know why our baby died. Many women wonder what they did to cause their baby to die. They dwell on whether something they ate hurt their baby, or whether that glass of wine they had before they knew they were pregnant caused them to miscarry. I remember traveling to the celebration of life for a friend a week or so before I found out my third baby had died. It was a long, uncomfortable car ride, and I didn't get much sleep that weekend. Did the stress or lack of sleep cause my miscarriage? Was it somehow my fault?

Just like we still can't cure the common cold, science and the medical community don't really help much. We don't have a lot of answers about why miscarriage happens. The uncertainty around miscarriage can be something that is terrifying, because it means that we can't predict if we're going to lose our baby. It's like getting pregnant itself - something really important to most of us, but something that working hard at doesn't seem to influence the end result.

I've spoken with women who are convinced that nothing they did caused their miscarriage, and nothing they could have done would have saved their baby. I've also talked with women who almost seem to NEED to blame themselves. It was definitely something they did, and they're not only grieving the loss of their baby, they're also struggling with guilt. My heart aches in many ways for these women who are blaming themselves, usually over something that most of the time wouldn't have had any impact on a healthy pregnancy and baby.

Still, I usually don't try to change a woman's mind if she believes she caused her miscarriage. I see the need to take responsibility for a miscarriage as one of the only ways that we can regain some sense of control over the extremely important yet unpredictable nature of pregnancy and childbirth. If we caused it, then maybe we can change our behaviour so that it doesn't happen again.

Unfortunately, gaining a sense of control sometimes means we are also taking the blame and beating ourselves up for something that we really didn't influence - and that we can't change moving forward.

> That's the Control Myth - that we can deal with the fear of uncertainty by controlling things. **Trying to control the uncontrollable results in even more stress and fear.**

Is Parenting an Exception?

Byron Katie is an interesting woman, and teaches some interesting lessons. I'm paraphrasing here, but one of her main lessons is that suffering comes when we're in someone else's business. We have our own business (the things we can control), other people have their business, and then there's a category of stuff that's God's or the Universe's business. We can control what we eat, whether we exercise, and if we go to the doctor for checkups and when we feel ill. But ultimately, whether we get sick isn't totally in our control.

I see this idea of everyone having their own "business" as relevant to the question about whether it's helpful to see parenting as trying to change our children (this is an adaptation of Byron Katie's ideas by me - not sure if she has ever said this or not!). When we're handed our newborn, their business pretty much consists of pooping, peeing, breathing, crying, and flailing their body. Basic stuff like that. Where they go, what they wear, what they eat - that's pretty much up to us as their parent. That stuff starts out as our business.

I see raising kids as gradually letting them take over their own business - or being forced to! When we try to get our kids to do stuff, we're acting as if those things are our business. Sometimes they are, and sometimes it would be more helpful to start passing those things off. I also do see it as a parent's responsibility to try to teach their children their values - but whether the child ends up living by them isn't really in their parent's control, in the end.

The Control Question

So here's the question - what part of the thing you want to accomplish is in your control? We talked about this a bit in the Starting to Redefine Success section near the beginning of the book. If you're wanting to feel you are a successful parent, making that dependent on the behaviour of your child could backfire. So what about being a great parent is in your control? Is there a behaviour of YOURS you want to stop? Start? Do more often?

Doing sales calls as an entrepreneur can also be a good example. If you have a goal related to making a certain amount of money or number of sales, that's not totally up to you. Someone else has to say yes for you to make a sale! What you can control are things like how many calls you make a day, and how many networking meetings you go to in a week.

This question can be asked of anything you've decided is part of success for you.

Five Growing Questions about Control:

1. How comfortable are you with unpredictability in general?

2. What are some ways you benefit from how you deal with unpredictability?

3. What are some ways that how you deal with unpredictability hurts you?

4. Does "everything can be redeemed" sit better with you than "everything happens for a reason"? Why or why not?

5. What is one thing you try to control in your life that you can see isn't really (or not totally) in your control? What would it take to let go of the illusion of control? What would happen if you did?

Control Summary Question:

What was one thing you learned in this chapter about control that you want to include in your personal definition of success? Write or dictate a note for yourself, or put it in the appropriate section of the journal provided (find out how to download the journal for free at http://tamsen.ca/paradoxjournalfree).

Happy people plan actions, they don't plan results.

- Dennis Waitley

Redefine Success: Make Success NOW

The foolish man seeks happiness in the distance, the wise grows it under his feet.

- James Oppenheim

Many people approach success as if it has to be made up of huge accomplishments.

Major life events such as graduating from university, getting married, having a child, getting a great job or promotion, buying your first house - those are often the things that we list when we are asked what success is. But that means we have to put off feeling successful for quite awhile, often for years. As discussed in The Paradox of Success chapter, we convince ourselves "I'll finally be happy WHEN…" Yet we may never get there. And it often leaves us feeling hollow if we do.

Wouldn't it be better to intentionally create a life where you get to feel successful almost every day? Not only does it mean there's the possibility that you could feel successful NOW, but if you're off track you have the chance to figure it out before you invest years in something that won't fulfill you.

If you've gone through the exercises and answered the questions in this book, you're well on the way to understanding your values, passions, and purpose. Let's work to figure out how you can incorporate those things into your life NOW.

Create Daily Practices

Deliberately creating daily practices - you might think of them as habits - that add to your feelings of success and fulfillment can be huge in creating a life you enjoy living. This can be as simple as creating time every day to do things that bring you joy. I have multiple scheduled events weekly where I connect with friends. I'm still struggling to keep up my daily journalling practice, but I always feel better when I do it.

What things can you schedule into your routine to help you feel successful and satisfied?

If you're unsure where to start, two of the practices that many people find helpful are practicing gratitude and practicing self-compassion. If you already journal or meditate, consider making gaining clarity about what you should work on a focus of your practice for awhile. If you don't already journal or meditate, those are great things to try! If you'd like help getting started journalling, you can check out my Journalling Jumpstart course at http://tamsen.ca/journallingjumpstart.

Build Celebrating Success into Your Day

Scheduling fulfilling things into your day can certainly help you feel successful - but including a chance to acknowledge that you are successful is important too.

Have you ever accomplished a really big goal - and then it just felt like - NEXT!?

Often accomplishments that are huge and have taken years, like graduating from university, are celebrated at an event, maybe a family dinner, and then - "So, when are you getting a job, anyway?"

I've mentioned that running my Guelph Moms Supporting Moms Facebook group is one of the things that helps me to feel successful every day. That group wouldn't exist if not for me, and it's a community where moms help each other and show incredible courage and kindness. I spend a fair bit of time in that group every day, and when I go to bed at night I often pause and enjoy the feeling of success I get from being the main one who has created and maintains that "container".

How can you build celebration into your day?

Five Growing Questions about Feeling Successful Now:

1. Is there a big goal you're working toward with the feeling "I'll be happy when..." - can you make this something you can bring into the present?

2. How do you recharge your batteries? Can you schedule this daily?

3. What is an area of your life where you want to feel more successful? Can you build steps to reach this goal into your daily routine?

4. When's the last time you celebrated some part of your success? What was it, how did you celebrate, and what did the celebration feel like?

5. How can you schedule time - even just a moment to reflect - to celebrate your successes daily?

Feeling Successful Now Summary Question:

What was one thing you learned in this chapter about feeling successful now that you want to include in your personal definition of success? Write or dictate a note for yourself, or put it in the appropriate section of the journal provided (find out how to download the journal for free at http://tamsen.ca/paradoxjournalfree).

When you recover or discover something that nourishes your soul and brings joy, care enough about yourself to make room for it in your life.

- Jean Shinoda Bolen

The Beginning, NOT the End

> He who would learn to fly one day must first learn to stand and walk and run and climb and dance; one cannot fly into flying.
>
> - Nietzsche

So - we've talked about the Paradox of Success - why many of us are "successful", yet feel anything but.

We've gone through why it's important to create self-worth, healthy relationships, and a life full of meaning if you're going to feel successful. Along the way, we've discussed 15 curiosities of confidence, happiness, and healing that might trip you up as you redefine success for yourself.

Now we're at the end of the book, you have answered some challenging questions that have provided a foundation for you to redefine success for yourself.

Personally, I consider redefining success a lifelong journey, which is why I believe this book is the beginning, not the end.

It is natural as you move forward in this journey, you will gain clarity, and also that you will change - and so will what success means to you. That's totally normal and ok! I hope that as you move forward this book will help you figure out what you want, how to feel successful, and inspire you to share your journey with others.

Bringing it Together

So you've answered some important questions for yourself that will help you create a life you WANT to live.

In this section I'm going to get you to put some things in one place and then decide on the next step forward.

If you've done these exercises and answered these questions, this will just be a matter of bringing things together here - and if you don't have these answers yet, then you know your next steps are answering the questions.

1. My top 2 values are: ______________________________ and ______________________________.

2. One way I want to see my values reflected more in my life is: ____.

3. Passions I want to have more of in my life are: ____.

4. My purpose statement is: It should be easier to ____________________________ than to ________________________.

5. My soul family includes ________________, ____________________, and __________________. (May be more or less than 3!)

6. Someone I want to create better boundaries with is _________________________.

7. The universal need I want more of right now is ____________________________.

8. A major "Ah-ha" that I got from reading my 16 Personalities type is that to feel successful I need ___________________________________.

9. My main love language is ____________________________ so to feel loved and valued, I'm going to ask (person) ______________________ for (action) ______________________ (be as specific as possible).

10. Go back to the Creating Self Worth Summary chapter, question #3. What is the main thing you want to change about your self-worth? Don't be afraid to change your answer.

11. Go back to the Creating Healthy Relationships Summary chapter, question #3. What is the main thing you want to change about the health of your relationships? Don't be afraid to change your answer.

12. Go back to the Creating Meaning Summary chapter, question #3. What is the main thing you want to change about the level of meaning you have in your life? Again, don't be afraid to change your answer.

13. Of all these things we've just brought together, what feels the most important to you right now is: ________________________________. Explore why.

Now Make an Action Plan

Ok, so here's where you commit to doing something!

Remember a few things.

First, this doesn't have to be an immense, earth shattering change. It's better to start small and get some momentum than try to make a huge change and get discouraged because you don't see much progress.

Second, set a time limit to do a review - try this for anywhere from a week to a month, then check in with yourself to see how it's going. Remember that if something scares you it might be because it's new, which is ok. If you start feeling like something is challenging your values, consider rereading the Paradox of Fear chapter and figuring out whether this is a fear you should listen to or a fear you should work past.

Third, there are multiple ways of choosing something to be the first area of change (question #1 below) - it could be the one that you think is the most important (question #13 from the last section), the area where you think you'd see the biggest results the fastest, the easiest, the most fun - whatever seems reasonable to you. Remember not to try to maximize, good enough to move forward is good enough!

Fourth, keeping a journal or other notes along the way can help you notice the progress you're making and the challenges you face. Small steps can result in huge changes over time - consider how you will keep track of your progress so you can celebrate!

Fifth, remember to practice patience and self-compassion.

1. The first area in my life I am going to choose to feel more successful in is ______________________.

2. Something that I can do that's in my control about (#1) is ______________________.

3. A way that I can do (#2) (almost) every day is ____________________________________.

4. A way that I'm going to celebrate doing (#2) daily is ___________________________.

5. The main challenge I expect to have doing (#2) is ______________________.

6. In addition to practicing self-compassion, another thing I will do to support myself in this adventure as I accomplish (#2) is ________________________________.

7. When I run into trouble, I will ask (person) ____________________ for help, including asking for emotional support if I need it.

The road to success is always under construction.

- Lily Tomlin

What to Do if You're Still Struggling to Feel Successful

Do not sit still; start moving now. In the beginning, you may not go in the direction you want, but as long as you are moving, you are creating alternatives and possibilities.

- Rodolfo Costa

I've shared my best tips and wisdom I've acquired here to help you create your own personal definition of success. That's a critical step so you can FEEL successful now and every day.

Sometimes you can see results quickly with some of these strategies, but sometimes it does take time. Remember to practice self-compassion!

If you're still feeling stuck or you feel you need more help, I don't want to leave you hanging.

Of course, me writing a book and putting it out there isn't the same thing as being present for you, listening to you, and customizing my suggestions for you personally. If you're interested in that kind of help, and you'd like me to be the one to help you feel successful, you can check out the "work with me" tab on my website, https://www.tamsenconnects.com to see my current offerings, or reach out to me at tamsen@tamsenconnects.com.

That being said, there are several ways in my experience that people get stuck, and I'd like to help you through them here. Are any of these things your main challenge right now?

#1 - You Need to be Heard

It's a very human need to feel heard and understood before you move forward in trying to solve your problems. You don't necessarily need to pay a professional to listen to you. If you develop true friendships, what I call your soul family, they will help you, and you can help them in return.

I deal with this topic extensively in The Paradox of Support chapter. If you feel that this might be your main challenge, that you feel lonely, disconnected, and don't feel that anyone understands you, consider rereading that chapter and following the advice there.

#2 - You're Struggling for Clarity

Sometimes we just can't see what we can't see, and we need another set of eyes.

If you can identify with other people who are experiencing the paradox of success, but you're just not sure what you're really struggling with, you may benefit from an outside perspective. I'll share with you some of the questions I've asked people to help them get clarity, they might help you too. You might want to work through these on your own. It can also be really helpful to discuss these questions with a friend you trust to get a bit of that outside perspective:

1. Is there a time in your life where you felt successful (the way you want to feel now)? If so, tell a detailed story about that time. Include as many details as you can to get clues, and dig into those details to figure out what contributed to your feelings of success. What about the situation was important? Who you were with? What impact you had? How large your impact was? The fact you were challenged? Did you have to learn something? What else was going on in your life at the time? I highly recommend writing this down and then going back and digging through it for clues. Once you have some ideas about what you might be missing now, consider how you can add some of those things into your life.

2. Are you trying to control something that just isn't in your control? Reread the Redefine Success: Make Success in Your Control chapter on control and see if what you're trying to change is in your control. If you're trying to change something that you don't have power over, do your best to

figure out how to make changes that can help you that are in your control.

3. Are you blocked from realizing what success is for you because you're resisting letting go of what you've been told success is, or you've been told things that bring you joy and fulfillment aren't worthwhile? You might find it useful to review Curiosity #11 - The One Passion Myth, particularly Susan's story of building a life and business around passions and a purpose that she was told as a child weren't valuable or meaningful. Curiosity #12 - Truth Bomb: We Undervalue our Talents could also give you some key insights. If you skipped over the questions in those chapters, or didn't devote some serious attention to them, consider going back and really digging deep into your passions and talents.

4. I highly recommend starting a journalling practice if you don't already have one. You don't have to write, you can do an audio or video journal. It can be a hugely helpful way of connecting with yourself. There is a lot of power in having to put things into words, and it often can reveal where you're unclear and what you can work on. You can use journalling to help you answer the questions above, and it is something that can help you recognize your progress and help you in many other ways.

#3 - You're Overwhelmed and Don't Know Where to Start

If you're feeling like a lot of these things could help and you're paralyzed with indecision about where to start or what might help you most - you're experiencing the paradox of options (remember Curiosity #14)!

Here are some suggestions:

1. Realize that there's probably no "wrong" choice. Remember the satisficing strategy from the Paradox of Options chapter (Curiosity #14 - The Paradox of Options)? Choose something that's good enough and use that to move forward. Don't worry about maximizing and choosing the absolutely best thing of all options, or you'll likely stay stuck. Prioritize taking action and getting some forward momentum! This is an important point: Don't be afraid of making a mistake. Even moving in the wrong direction gives you more information than standing still does, and gets you unstuck.

2. Work on your self-compassion. Review Curiosity #2 - The Paradox of Self-Compassion if you need to. Almost everyone can hugely benefit from having more self-compassion, and it often adds to the effectiveness of anything else you try.

3. You can sign up for my weekly tips emails, which gives you one thing to try per week to see a bit of progress and gain momentum without overwhelm. You can sign up for those tips at tamsen.ca/confidencetips.

4. Reach out to me to see if we'd be a good fit to work together. One of the programs I currently offer is an hour long session called the Confidence Power Hour. In that program I scaffold you so you get clarity about your main challenge and you leave with only 1 or 2 things to try, so you can avoid the overwhelm. Because I'm working with you directly, we can make sure that the action items you leave with fit your personality and lifestyle. You can find out more about the Confidence Power Hour at tamsen.ca/confidencepowerhour. Of course, you can look at my other programs, or if you'd rather work with a different professional, reach out to them.

#4 - You Have Chosen to Do Something - And Can't Stick with it

Keeping momentum and motivation can be tough. Life happens and interrupts our best laid plans.

Another free online test that I recommend for people that I work with is called the Four Tendencies by Gretchen Rubin. You can find it at tamsen.ca/4tendencies. The main benefit of this test is to give insights about how you respond to expectations. We have expectations for ourselves (what she calls internal expectations) and others have expectations for us (what she calls external expectations). Do you tend to try to meet both of those types of expectations, one more than another, or neither? If you're like a lot of people, you're what's called an "Obliger". If that's you, you can relate to wanting to meet other people's expectations, and they come before promises you've made to yourself.

You tend to let yourself down.

One of the best ways to get around this is to turn something you're trying to do for yourself into something you're doing with someone else. If you've ever had a gym buddy or otherwise exercised with someone else and that helps you stick to your plan, then this is likely to help you. Find a friend who either wants to do this journey with you, or support you in your journey, and schedule regular meetings where you discuss your progress since last time, and set a goal for next time. Being able to reach out to them in between if you're struggling to stay on track can be a huge bonus too!

Finding a friend to support you is one of the best ways to make external accountability, but there are other ways too. Of course you could hire a coach or other professional to regularly check in with and keep you on track. Having accountability is an advantage of participating in a group experience, whether it's something paid, or something informal like a book club. If you're interested in seeing what group experiences I have coming up related to this book, you can check out my books page on my website at https://www.tamsenconnects.com/books. There are also online options like StickK, which allow you to make a customized "contract" with yourself, and offers options like having a referee, making your progress public to your family and friends, or having a monetary penalty if you fail to meet your goal. You can check out StickK at tamsen.ca/stickk (note I'm not an affiliate and I haven't tried this program myself because this isn't where I typically get stuck).

If you aren't an Obliger or having an accountability buddy doesn't feel like enough, consider learning more about your Tendency and what Gretchen Rubin believes will motivate you.

> You don't have to see the whole staircase, just take the first step.
>
> - Martin Luther King, Jr.

Additional Resources

Yes, your transformation will be hard. Yes, you will feel frightened, messed up, and knocked down. Yes, you'll want to stop. Yes, it's the best work you'll ever do.

- Robin Sharma

I've mentioned some of these throughout the book, but I wanted to bring together resources in a separate section for those of you who are keen to dig deeper into some of the topics we discussed here.

Resources
Created for Readers of this Book

Some resources that can help you get more out of this book:

- I've created additional resources for this book, and I'll be adding to them as time goes on. You can find them on my website at https://tamsenconnects.com/paradox

- I created a digital download with the questions from this book. It brings all the questions together in a journal so you can keep them organized in one place. You can find out how to get it for free as a fillable pdf at http://tamsen.ca/paradoxjournalfree

Other Relevant Resources by Me

Some of these resources are explicitly mentioned in the book, and some are supplementary resources for people who would like more evidence for the ideas presented here, and to dig deeper. Most of these are to do with aspects of emotional health.

- If you're interested in keeping up with what other books I'm writing, you do that at https://www.tamsenconnects.com/books

- You can find the Momtellectual Podcast at https://www.tamsenconnects.com/momtellectual, on YouTube, or through your favourite podcast provider.

- If you're interested in bite-sized suggestions for increasing your confidence and feelings of success every week, you can sign up for my weekly tips at tamsen.ca/confidencetips

Relevant Resources by Others

These are resources I have found useful and interesting. I'm not an affiliate or otherwise getting anything from you checking them out, I think they're potentially useful, so enjoy!

- An article written for the general public summarizing the findings of Dr. Kristin Neff and Dr. Christopher Germer about the benefits of "mindful self-compassion" can be found at https://www.mindful.org/the-transformative-effects-of-mindful-self-compassion/

- A TED talk about why it's important to acknowledge and accept all of our emotions is "Leaving the cult of happiness" by Keely Herron which can be found at https://www.youtube.com/watch?v=xnovQVRHj5c

- John Cacioppo and William Patrick's book Loneliness: Human Nature and the Need for Social Connection is a very important deep dive into loneliness including where loneliness comes from, it's impacts on our health, and how to stop being lonely and feel connected to other people.

- There is a TON of research that our decisions aren't really ruled by logic, but that being able to make decisions at all is largely an emotional process. Antonio Damasio's book Descartes' Error: Emotion, Reason, and the Human Brain is a very readable example of this research.

- Byron Katie is an interesting woman, and she teaches some interesting lessons. I'm paraphrasing here, but one of her main lessons is that suffering comes when we're in someone else's business. We have our own business (the things we can control), other people have their business, and then there's a category of stuff that's God's or the Universe's business. Check out her stuff if you're interested in digging deeper into her philosophy. There are lots of ways you can find out more, including books on Amazon and video interviews you can find by searching online.

- Here is the list of "universal" needs I used in this book. It was created by the Center for Nonviolent Communication and can be found at (https://www.cnvc.org/). Note that they ask the reference to this to include:

(c) 2005 by Center for Nonviolent Communication
Website: www.cnvc.org Email: cnvc@cnvc.org
Phone: +1.505-244-4041

- If you're interested in how food affects our weight and health, I strongly recommend looking into Jonathan Bailor's

"The Calorie Myth". It's available as a book, a course on CreativeLive, and there are lots of resources online.

- If you want to hear more about courage and how to develop more of it, check out the work of Mel Robbins. She has a CreativeLive course, and multiple books.

- If you are interested in aspects of confidence and how lack of confidence can hold women back at work, I recommend the book The Confidence Code by Katty Kay and Claire Shipman.

Emotional Health Resources

I gave you some resources for emotional health earlier, but since this is the resources section I thought I would also add them here:

- Brené Brown. Seriously. Check out her stuff - she is an awesome researcher storyteller who focuses on the importance of emotions, love, and belonging. She has a couple of amazing TED talks and books, a blog, lots of amazing stuff.

- The Grief Recovery Method Handbook is also another great place to get more information. Grief is a reaction to any change, and it is not one emotion, but is an emotional experience that can encompass any and all emotions. I highly recommend learning about how to be emotionally safe and healthy, and this is a great system to use. They also have a website with a lot of blog posts that are great resources.

- For an exploration of what each individual emotion and emotional experience might be trying to tell you, check out "The Language of Emotions: What Your Feelings Are Trying to Tell You" by Karla McLauren. I don't necessarily agree with everything she says, but her book is really interesting and provoked me to lots of thinking.

At any given moment you have the power to say: This is not how the story is going to end.

- Christine Mason Miller

Consider Connecting

I define connection as the energy that exists between people when they feel seen, heard, and valued; when they can give and receive without judgment; and when they derive sustenance and strength from the relationship.

- Brené Brown

Thank you so much for being open to the adventure of creating your own personal definition of success. I believe that creating your own personal definition of success is a critical step toward you feeling successful, and if you do the work laid out here you will be well on your way to creating a life you love to live.

If you are excited by this topic, or if you have questions and I can help you on your way, I would love to connect. Here are some ways you can find me:

- My main website is https://www.tamsenconnects.com and my main email is tamsen@tamsenconnects.com. Feel free to reach out!
- Keep up to date with what additional resources I'm creating for readers of this book at https://www.tamsenconnects.com/paradox.
- Keep up to date with other books that I'm creating and launching at https://www.tamsenconnects.com/books.
- Remember you can get the free digital journal that accompanies this book at http://tamsen.ca/paradoxjournalfree.
- My main business FB page is at https://www.facebook.com/TamsenConnects.
- If you're a mom local to me in the Guelph area and aren't already a member, you may be interested in checking out Guelph Moms Supporting Moms, at https://www.facebook.com/groups/GuelphMomsSupportingMoms.
- If you're a mom local to me in the Guelph area and have a business or a side gig, you might want support in your

business and you can join Guelph Business Moms at https://www.facebook.com/groups/GuelphBusinessMoms.

- I'm on LinkedIN at https://www.linkedin.com/in/tamsentaylor. Please note I'm not there all that often!

Thanks for reading, and I hope this book has helped you! Feedback is welcome at any of the communication channels mentioned here.

> We are like islands in the sea, separate on the surface but connected in the deep.
>
> - William James

Acknowledgements

Story is the umbilical cord that connects us to the past, present, and future. Family. Story is a relationship between the teller and the listener, a responsibility...Story is an affirmation of our ties to one another.

- Terry Tempest Williams

Thank you to everyone who supported me in getting this book written and published!

Thank you to my soul family, Audrey, Theresa, and Shanan. Your contributions are obvious since you appear in many of the stories here! I not only wouldn't have had nearly as much fun writing and publishing this book without you, but I wouldn't have survived this far into the pandemic with my emotional health and sense of humour (mostly) intact.

I've explored these ideas in too many conversations to remember, much less mention. If you've been part of those I thank you deeply for your insights and the fun we've had. I especially think of Marisa, Belinda, Danielle, Shilpa, Megan, Kimberley, Steph, Rachel, Mimi, Jackie, Christine, and Eleni.

Thanks to Leigh and Marilyn for sharing your book writing and publishing savvy.

Thank you to the amazing interviewees who have been my guests on the Momtellectual Podcast. You help us all feel less alone by sharing your stories, and you are the source of a lot of the wisdom I share in this book.

Thank you to the members of my Guelph Moms Supporting Moms and Guelph Business Moms Facebook groups. I wouldn't feel nearly as successful without the joy of creating and maintaining the communities in which you support and cheer on one another. Special thanks to Robin-Lee and Vanessa, my co-leaders. I'm grateful I don't have to lead alone.

Thanks to my graduate advisor, Steve. You took more than one chance on me, and had my back. I'm extremely grateful. Thanks to my mentor, Albert. I don't think I would have been able to love teaching without your guidance.

Thanks to my mom Joyce, my son Tommy, and my husband David. Mom, I miss you, and hope we can get together again soon! Darn pandemic. Tommy and David, being locked down brought us closer, and for that the pandemic hasn't been all bad.

And thanks to my dad. I miss you. You were the best storyteller I've ever met, and I hope I have reflected some of your talent here.

You can't heal the people you love. You can't make choices for them. You can't rescue them. You can promise that they won't journey alone. You can loan them your map. But this trip is theirs.

- Laura Jean Truman

CPSIA information can be obtained
at www.ICGtesting.com
Printed in the USA
LVHW021921090922
728003LV00001B/110